To Love as
God Loves

Roberta C. Bondi

To Love as God Loves

Conversations with the
Early Church

Fortress Press   Philadelphia

Material from *Dorotheus of Gaza: Discourses and Sayings*, translated and introduction by Eric P. Wheeler, copyright 1977 by Cistercian Publications, Inc., Kalamazoo, Michigan, is reprinted by permission.

Material from *The Sayings of the Desert Fathers: The Alphabetical Collection*, translated by Benedicta Ward, S.L.G., copyright 1981 by A. R. Mowbray & Co., Ltd., is reprinted by permission. Permission is also granted by Cistercian Publications, Inc.

Chapter 3 is a revised and expanded version of "Humility: A Meditation on an Ancient Virtue for Modern Christians," which originally appeared in *Quarterly Review*, vol. 3, no. 4 (Winter 1983), copyright by the United Methodist Publishing House and the United Methodist Board of Higher Education and Ministry.

Psalm 126 is copyright © 1963 by Ladies of the Grail (England). Used by permission of G.I.A. Publications, Inc., Chicago, Illinois, exclusive agent. All rights reserved.

Biblical quotations, unless otherwise noted, are from the Revised Standard Version of the Bible, copyright 1946, 1952, ©1971, 1973 by the Division of Christian Education of the National Council of the Churches of Christ in the U.S.A., and are used by permission.

Contents

Preface

I first met the men and women I am writing about in this book twenty years ago. I was a graduate student at the time, and though I was struggling with Christianity, I had not yet found a form of it that could draw both my heart and my head to God. I did not know why this was so, but I knew that it was. One day, sitting in the library, I began to read a collection of sermons written by a sixth-century representative of this tradition, Philoxenus of Mabbug, and I started to see glimpses of what it might mean to be a Christian, to love God and other human beings, to pray. Over the intervening years I have met as many others of this tradition as I could, and I have found in them a real fleshing out of what Christian love is: God's for all of us, ours for each other, God's world, and God. Their warmth, insights, helpfulness have been a continuous source of life for me, the greatest gift I have ever received. I believe in our modern world, in which it is so hard even to know what being a Christian might mean, they may also be a gift for you.

I have had much help with writing this book over the years. Though Derwas Chitty is dead now, he was the first person who gave me a hint of what this Christianity was like. From Rod Hunter and Don Saliers came the encouragement to try to write the book, as well as a willingness to read through the manuscript in various stages. Bob Ratcliff and Jan Stephens followed the whole and gave extremely helpful insights. Melissa Walker, Bob Perry, O.P., Martin Iott, O.P., Mary Ann Ennis, O.P., and Marie Bogert contributed a great deal more than they will ever know by being there and being who they are. My mother provided the computer which made the writing possible. Most of all, I want to thank Richard, my husband, who was a constant conversation partner and a continuous source of physical and emotional support and love.

Chapter 1

Beginnings

Many of us who call ourselves Christian long to be what we call ourselves, but we cannot see how to do it, granted our culture's basic assumptions about what it means to be a human being. If we assume with our culture that the goal of human life is individual self-development, how does this goal leave space for love that might thwart that development? How does the need for assertiveness in a world that despises the weak fit with the Christ who "did not count equality with God a thing to be grasped, but emptied himself, taking the form of a servant" (Phil. 2:6–7)? How does an ethos of productivity fit with the image of the cross? We suspect that our culture's assumptions about human life may be wrong but it is hard to see what alternative options we have.

This book is intended to open a dialogue on just such topics between you, the reader, and some fascinating figures from the early period of the church. Though these men and women in many significant ways lived in a culture very different from our own, many of the problems they faced were surprisingly similar to ours. Common sense seemed to conflict with Christian vision just as much for them as it does for us. The virtues they espoused were as countercultural and as open to misinterpretation then as they are now, as a little saying of Abba John the Dwarf, preserved in the Sayings of the Fathers, illustrates. Perhaps this interchange occurred when a disciple complained to his teacher about the apparently unrealistic nature of humility.

Abba John said, "Who sold Joseph?" A brother replied saying, "It was his brethren." The old man said to him, "No, it was his humility which sold him, because he could have said, 'I am their brother' and have objected, but, because he kept silence, he sold himself by his humility. *It is also his humility which set him up as chief in Egypt."* (Apoth., John the Dwarf 20, p. 90. Italics added.)

They believed, in spite of society's pressures, that love is the goal of the Christian life and humility is what it takes to bring us toward it. Love and humility were not the pious attitudes of idealistic but impractical men and women who could not cope with "real life." Rather, as they understood them, love and humility provide human beings with a realistic and powerful way of disarming such a violent society as theirs and ours. Without them, they believed that life dissipates into nothing, and, paradoxically, the self and its power to act are lost altogether. Only as we learn to love God and others do we gain real freedom and autonomy in a society in which most people live in a state of slavery to their own needs and desires.

The dialogue to be opened here is intended to be a real one, however, and we must acknowledge that our dialogue partners are in fundamental ways very different from us. They are men and women from the past. Most of them lived in the Near East, in Egypt or Palestine or Syria, in the fourth through sixth centuries. All of them were among the first generations of Christians who decided that they could best love God and their neighbor by living a different Christian life from the one most of their fellow Christians lived in the world. Their science, philosophy, medicine, and psychology differed from ours. Many of their presuppositions and conclusions are ones we will vigorously reject, sometimes on the grounds that they violate our own biblical understanding of God, the world, and ourselves.

We should not expect that these people, so distant from ourselves, would share our perspectives even in fundamental places. We do not ask them for authoritative dogmatic answers to our modern problems. We do ask them—and they give what we ask—for some of their insights into Christian life, presented to us in such a way that we may mull them over, consider them, use them, or discard them as they speak to us. The agenda of ancient Christians is not always ours. Here is where we must remember that this is to be a dialogue, a back-and-forth movement between our agenda and theirs. They must be free to tell it as they see it; we must not always expect to agree or even like what they have to say.

On the other hand, this book is not intended to be a catalogue of everything they believed, along with the reasons they believed it. I have selected topics for discussion that seem to have particular relevance to the modern reader. What they have to say about the way in which our attitudes toward food orient us toward the world are thought-provoking and well worth considering. On the other hand, the conviction that "one hour of sleep [a night] is enough" for a person completely devoted to the Christian life strikes us as bizarre enough not to merit serious consideration at all.

Certainly, these texts do not speak with a single voice, anyway. The material we will be using in our dialogue is varied; there is no single voice from the past. Partly, this is because there is so much material that has survived from our Christian past. There is an enormous variety in the kind of materials themselves: we will be using biographies, sermons, letters, collections of sayings and stories, dialogues, biblical commentaries, and essays from a period of about three hundred years.

Even more important, however, was the conviction of these men and women that, while Christians share a common goal, and in many respects a common way of life, there is no one single right route everyone must follow to get there. People are different from each other; what keeps me from being able to love is probably very different from what hinders you. What corrects my lack of love may only make your situation worse.

Because they took the necessity of diversity so seriously, one text sometimes even seems to contradict another. For example, one father (or Abba, as the teacher was called) regards hospitality as the basic Christian discipline; his best friend believes it to be silence. There is a little tale about these two men, Abba Moses and Abba Arsenius, commenting upon their different ways, and how each was blessed of God. The story was told that a visitor to Egypt wished to see the two famous teachers, Arsenius and Moses. Arriving at the house of Arsenius, he went in and sat down. Arsenius ignored him, and after a while, he asked to be taken to Moses. Moses was glad to see him, visited with him, and sent him off with happiness. Another person heard him and prayed, saying,

"Lord, explain this matter to me: for Thy name's sake the one flees from [human beings] and the other, for Thy name's sake, receives them with open arms." Then two large boats were shown to him on a river and he saw Abba Arsenius and the Spirit of God sailing in the one, in perfect peace; and in the other was Abba Moses with the angels of God, and they were all eating honey cakes. (Apoth., Arsenius 38, pp. 17–18)

Another saying puts the same point more tersely:

> Abba Poemen said that Abba John said that the saints are like a group of trees, each bearing different fruit, but watered from the same source. The practices of one saint differ from those of another, but it is the same Spirit that works in all of them. (Apoth., John the Dwarf 43, p. 95)

The following pages are not intended to offer a dogmatic picture of "Christian life, its meaning and practice." As we would suspect from the two sayings above, even in the period in which they were written down the ancient texts were not meant to "lay down the law" for their readers or hearers. Only scripture could do that. Instead, these texts are intended to offer some new ways for the reader to understand what it could mean to be a human being made in the image of God. Certainly, the following pages are meant to offer the reader a way into these fascinating texts that belong to our common Christian heritage.

READING THE EARLY TEXTS

In most of this early literature, love as the goal of the Christian life is not referred to directly. Instead, it is taken for granted, and if the reader does not remember that love is the goal, he or she may find the literature very confusing. For example, the word "love" does not appear at all in the little saying "An angry person is not acceptable to God, even if that person should raise the dead." On the surface, such a statement might appear to be a legalistic judgment on the sinfulness of anger. In actual fact, however, it is a reminder that a Christian's first business is love of neighbor and God: even astounding works of piety or holiness count no more than "a noisy gong or a clanging cymbal" without love (1 Cor. 13:1).

Further, like Jesus' parables, a great deal of this material, especially from the collections of Sayings of the Fathers, does not make its points by means of propositional statements. Often the material makes only a partial statement, as the one above about anger does, or tells only part of a story. Instead, the reader is to draw her or his own conclusion about the meaning of a teacher's words. At other times, the actions of a teacher provide a drama from which the watchers are to draw their conclusions, as we see in the story told of Abba Moses, the great black monk who had been a highway robber in his former life:

A brother at Scetis committed a fault. A council was called to which Abba Moses was invited, but he refused to go to it. Then the priest sent someone to say to him, "Come, for everyone is waiting for you." So he got up and went. He took a leaking jug, filled it with water and carried it with him. The others came out to meet him and said to him, "What is this, Father?" The old man said to them, "My sins run out behind me, and I do not see them, and today I am coming to judge the errors of another." When they heard that they said no more to the brother but forgave him. (Apoth., Moses 2, p. 139)

This is teaching by the method of indirection, where the student must come to the student's own conclusion. In the ancient texts it has at least two stems. The first is the Bible: Nathan the prophet did not get David the king to understand what he had done in taking Bathsheba from Uriah the Hittite by preaching him a sermon on the virtues of loyalty and the evils of adultery. Instead he told him a story about a poor man who had one lamb and a rich man who had many, so that, while it was Nathan who said to him, "You are the man" (2 Sam. 12:7), David was forced to accept Nathan's judgment because he had made it himself. Jesus used this teaching method very often: in fact, to his opponents it seems to have constituted one of his most infuriating qualities.

The second source of this method of indirection lies in the way I believe this material was to be used. Hardly ever was it meant to be taken literally. I have already said that it was not to be read as a series of propositional statements on the Christian life. These early Christians had a dislike as powerful as any twentieth-century Christian's for rigid answers about what it meant to be Christian. I suspect that only very small portions of these texts at a time were to be read or recited, mulled over, ruminated over. The reader or hearer was to try on the words, images, and ideas, measuring them against the teaching of Jesus, and on that basis let them make their appeal to the heart. Such a response is asked of us in this statement, for example:

Abba Theodore . . . said, "If you are temperate, do not judge the fornicator, for you would then transgress the law just as much. And he who said, 'Do not commit fornication,' also said, 'Do not judge.'" (Apoth., Theodore 3, p. 80)

Sometimes scripture is quoted or explained as it is in the passage just quoted; as often it lies implicitly behind what is said, only visible to the ancient or modern reader who already knows the scripture.

But who were these people with whom we are to begin a dialogue? To answer this question, we have to go back before the end of the third century and the beginning of the fourth when we first meet them.

During the very early years of Christianity, at the time when the Roman Empire was officially pagan, a Christian knew that Christian behavior excluded participation in paganism. This meant that not only was public life with its expectation of the famous "pinch of incense" prohibited to Christians. Many careers were closed to Christians—such as serving in the army, being a school teacher or an actor or actress—because they somehow entailed supporting, teaching, or depicting pagan mythology.

Furthermore, at a more private level Christians adhered to a moral code often at odds with the codes of the world they lived in. They were very strict about sin. Even up until the fourth century in some parts of the empire, it was believed that baptism wiped out all sins committed before it, but after baptism a person could only sin once and expect forgiveness. Certainly in the minds of these early Christians there was a great distinction between being a good citizen and being a good Christian.

But the fourth century changed all that when, with the emperor Constantine and his successors, Christianity not only became legal, it became the favored religion of the empire. This new state of affairs was a mixed blessing. Now public churches could be built and worship take place openly without the threat of martyrdom. New problems arose, and the most serious of them we have with us to this day: the distinction between being a good citizen and a good Christian became blurred as Christians began to "do well by doing good."

But even before the coming of Constantine in the fourth century when Christians still experienced persecution, people were especially aware of the seriousness of the demand of Jesus that we be perfect as his Father in heaven is perfect. In a new way the conviction grew among many men and women that while it is not theoretically impossible to be a Christian and live an ordinary life in the world, surely only the exceptional person could make a go of it.

Out of this conviction Anthony, the man who was credited with being the founder of monasticism in antiquity, took up his new life. It was about A.D. 269 that the eighteen-year-old heir and only son of Egyptian farmers heard the story of the Rich Young Ruler who would be perfect read in church and responded to it as a special call to him. He sold most of his property and gave away its proceeds, leaving only a little for his own care and that of his sister. Soon after, he heard in church "Do not be anxious for tomorrow"; he sold the rest of what he had and gave over the care of his sister to a group of spinster ladies. Then he was ready to take up his new life. He went on to receive instruction on living what was then considered to be an appropriate life of Christian asceticism and discipline from some old men who lived near his little town, and later on he moved out into the desert to take up the life style of the first Christian hermit. All of this we may still read in his biography, written by a man who knew him—the great Alexandrian bishop and theologian, Athanasius.

Anthony started out as a solitary. He learned his disciplines from others, but he did not understand what he did as part of a group effort. Nevertheless, Anthony does not fit our standard picture of the hermit. Very quickly in his career he found himself visited by potential disciples. Even more, Anthony was a public figure; he did not remain in the desert with these disciples. At one point in his career he journeyed into the great city of Alexandria where he publicly encouraged the martyrs who were being tried and killed. Later in his long life, back in the desert, he was visited by soldiers, government officials, pagan priests and philosophers, local landowners and peasants. All of these came to him for advice on the affairs of the secular world as well as of the spiritual.

Slightly after Anthony another kind of life sprang up in Egypt, a deliberately communal style of living associated with the name of Pachomius. Pachomius, unlike Anthony, had been reared in a pagan household. According to his early biographers, his first encounter with Christians came after he had been conscripted into the army. At the age of twenty, he and a group of young men were seized to fight as "recruits" in Constantine's army. They were locked up in a tower at Thebes, apparently without supplies, and when a group of Christians came late in the day bringing food, drinks, and other necessities, it made an enormous impression on Pachomius. When he asked who Christians were, he was told,

> They are [people] who bear the name of Christ, the only begotten Son of God, and they do good to everyone, putting their hope on him who made heaven and earth and us [human beings]. (V.P., p. 300)

Pachomius was so struck with this that he prayed on the spot to

God that, if he were to return alive, he would become a Christian—
which he understood in the terms in which he first encountered
Christians. This prayer provides us with a good insight into Pachomius's own understanding of his work. He prayed,

> God, maker of heaven and earth, if you will look upon me in my
> lowliness . . . if you deliver me from this affliction, I will serve your
> will all the days of my life and, loving all [people], I will be their
> servant according to your command. (V.P., p. 300)

Pachomius was released. Eventually he founded the first real religious communities in Tabennesis, far up the Nile from where
Anthony was located. These were highly organized with a complex
social structure. They were quickly inhabited by people of many
nations.

In between Anthony's style of living and Pachomius's there was
another style where a few or more monks would come together to
learn their way of life from a teacher, their Abba. The pattern of
their lives would be determined by their individual Abba. What
we see of the first generations of monks at Scetis and Nitria, the
two most famous centers in Egypt which were not associated with
Pachomius, suggests a real variety in the dispositions and methods
of these Abbas. We have already briefly met the stern and silent
Arsenius, who had been a Roman nobleman in his former life, and
the hospitable Moses, who had been a highway robber in his. Others, like Macarius of Alexandria, were known for fantastic asceticism, or perhaps a habit of continuous wandering about or exceptional solitariness.

There were women who also took up this life. One of Pachomius's first monasteries was for women. Unfortunately, it is hard
to know much about these women. The collections of sayings and
stories we have were written by men; the literature that remains
comes from a monastic culture that discouraged exchanges between the sexes and looked upon women with hostility and suspicion. The sayings of a few women teachers, who are called
"Ammas" or mothers, are included in the collections of the Sayings
of the Fathers, and Palladius tells us of some admirable women
whom we hear of from other places, but very clearly the little we
have left is so fragmented that we can only grieve for the loss of
the rest.

This is at best only a brief sketch of the beginnings of the people
with whom we are to open our dialogue. What we are about in

this book, however, is not to look at the history of early monastic communities. Rather, we want to discover what they thought the Christian life was about and how they were to arrive at it, and then have some conversation about it from our modern perspective. What they thought about the Christian life, its goal of love and the way of humility cuts right across early monasticism in all its varieties in Egypt and in those places heavily influenced by it, for while there was a great difference in degrees of asceticism, in diet, in styles of housing and association with others, there was a common vision of the fundamentals of Christian life.

Of what did this common vision consist? Anthony had set out on his new life when he heard "If you would be perfect, go, sell what you possess and give to the poor, . . . and come, follow me." Perfection is a concept that appears over and over in a wide spectrum of early Christian literature, and our own suspicion of the very idea of perfection would have struck our Christian forebears as both odd and frightening. The gospel, after all, is clear in its demand for perfection.

They did not, however, mean by it some kind of heroic and cold adherence to a list of rules concerning Christian behavior, as we are inclined to mean. Certainly, they did not mean by human perfection an utter freedom from temptation. Indeed, not only was the Christian never free from temptation: they were convinced that those who seemed to be relatively free of it were the men and women God protects because God knows how little temptation they could withstand.

When they heard the commandment to "be perfect" they understood it to be another way of phrasing the one Great Commandment, "you shall love the Lord your God with all your heart, and with all your soul, and with all your mind . . . [and] your neighbor as yourself." To be a perfect human being, a human being the way God intends human beings to be, is to be a fully loving person, loving God, and every bit as important, loving God's image, the other people who share the world with us.

On one level, this notion of love and perfection is startling. We are accustomed to think of perfection as a bad word. In a psychological context, it suggests a compulsive person who is never satisfied with anything, who is nit-picking over details and tied up with guilt, and whose favorite pastime is catching other people in mistakes. In a theological context, it suggests a refusal to accept our sinfulness in the eyes of God. All in all, we believe it to be true when we say "to err is human." But on the contrary, for the sisters and brothers of the desert quite the reverse was true; for them, "to love is human; not to love is less than human."

How they conceived of this love is a different question, and one which will be taken up in the next chapter. It is to be hoped that you already suspect that their notion of love is as different from ours as their notion of perfection. As they understood it, an ability to love is the very goal of the Christian life, and if love is its goal, humility is the way to it.

If perfection is a difficult word for modern Christians, humility is even more so. Certainly it is necessary that we examine our very legitimate problems with it, and we will in chapter 3. In the meanwhile, suffice it to say that, for them, as perfection is commanded of us in scripture, so is humility. In fact, not only is it commanded: God in Christ has been set before us as our very model of it in Philippians 2.

But humility did not mean for them a continuous cringing, cultivating a low self-image, and taking a perverse pleasure in being always forgotten, unnoticed, or taken for granted. Instead, humility meant to them a way of seeing other people as being as valuable in God's eyes as ourselves. It was for them a relational term having to do precisely with learning to value others, whoever they were. It had to do with developing the kind of empathy with the weaknesses of others that made it impossible to judge others out of our own self-righteousness.

Humility as they understood it was not really a virtue as we tend to think of the virtues. It was an attitude of heart without which the virtues had no Christian context. There is a striking story illustrating this point:

> One day Abba Agathon questioned Abba Alonius saying, "How can I control my tongue so as to tell no more lies?" And Abba Alonius said to him, "If you do not lie, you prepare many sins for yourself." "How is that?" said he. The old man said to him, "Suppose two men have committed a murder before your eyes and one of them fled to your cell. The magistrate, seeking him, asks you, "Have you seen the murderer?" If you do not lie, you will deliver him to death. It is better for you to abandon him unconditionally to God, for he alone knows all things." (Apoth., Alonius 4, p. 35)

This is a shocking and difficult story to us, and we will return to it later. Furthermore, the word "humility" is not even mentioned in it. Nevertheless, it illumines what we intend to discuss here, for it is humility that reminds Agathon that the goal of the Christian life is love; it is not to acquire a set of personal qualities, such as truthfulness. Humility makes it possible to distinguish between legalism and love. It makes us flexible. It puts heart into truthfulness. It makes our forgiveness of ourselves and others possible.

Chapter 2 _____

Love

In the fourth century what called so many men and women away
from ordinary life in the world and into the desert was the command of Jesus: "Be perfect, as your heavenly Father is perfect"
(Matt. 5:48). Strangely enough from our modern perspective, this
commandment did not seem either repulsive or impossible to
them. To us, it suggests legalism, or it fills us with despair or
bafflement. For them, however, the commandment to be perfect
was simply another way of phrasing the Great Commandment:
"You shall love the Lord your God with all your heart, and with
all your soul, and with all your strength, and with all your mind;
and your neighbor as yourself" (Luke 10:27). What Jesus asked of
those who took up his life was perfect love.

For Anthony in the desert and the men and women who came
after him, perfect love is the goal of the Christian life. "Love one
another as I have loved you" (John 15:12). "He who does not love
abides in death" (1 John 3:14). "Faith, hope, and love . . . but the
greatest of these is love." God asked it, they wished to accomplish
it, and they knew it is possible because the very desire to love and
be loved is part of human nature. It is part of the image of God.
Loving is natural; it is unnatural not to love. Of course most human
beings fail to love or love badly a lot of the time. This is because
we are dominated by the fear of death and of our own physical
and emotional vulnerability, and by our ways of compensating for
this fear. We need power over other people. We are afraid of the
future. We suffer from envy, resentments, depression, hyperac-
tivity, and boredom.

Our fourth-century ancestors thought none of this was necessary. God has come to us and still comes to us in Jesus to overcome our fears, to break the hold our destructive ways of being have over us, and to restore our wounded and distorted humanness if we want it and are willing to seek it. This was the very purpose of the incarnation: we are shown the way back to the original image of God in which we were created and enabled to become really loving, truly human. This was the inspiration for the movement that became monasticism.

PERFECTION AND LEGALISM

All this talk of "perfect" love is bound to make us modern readers uneasy. We think that the very goal of "perfection" coupled with monastic discipline was bound to result in a rigid concern for rules and regulations, not perfect love. It is true that the distinction between having perfect love as the real goal of the Christian life and the disciplines designed to foster that love was sometimes lost. Some brothers and sisters probably never knew any better; others did what human beings of all periods do: they simply forgot their goal, confusing their means with their end. We find many stories warning against such a confusion. Here are two speakers, a famous monk/bishop, Epiphanius, and Hilarion, who is credited with founding Palestinian monasticism. Notice the indirect way Epiphanius reminds Hilarion that the goal of the Christian life has to do with love, not rules:

> One day Saint Epiphanius sent someone to Abba Hilarion with this request, "Come, let us see one another before we depart from the body." When he came, they rejoiced in each other's company. During their meal, they were brought a fowl; Epiphanius took it and gave it to Hilarion. Then the old man said to him, "Forgive me, but since I received the habit I have not eaten meat that has been killed." Then the bishop answered, "Since I took the habit, I have not allowed anyone to go to sleep with a complaint against me and I have not gone to rest with a complaint against anyone." The old man replied, "Forgive me, your way of life is better than mine." (Apoth., Epiphanius 4, p. 57)

No amount of pious behavior or Christian discipline can replace love.

The word "perfection" coupled with the Christian life suggests more to us than grim legalism, however. Everybody knows someone who really believes he or she is nearly perfect, at least perfect enough to comment upon other people's imperfections. These people are difficult enough as it is without suggesting to them that actual perfection is a real possibility. Yet believing one is perfect enough to criticize others is self-righteousness, the sin of the Pharisee in the temple, not perfection. Self-righteousness is the opposite of love. Jesus attacked it repeatedly, and the monks were faithful to Jesus at this point. No amount of "goodness" puts a person in a position to render judgment on another's sin. Only God can do this. Growth toward perfect love in fact moves us increasingly into a deeper compassion for other people's human frailty. Love makes us less critical as we identify with others. When you see someone sin, says one of the Abbas, say, "Oh, Lord, he today, I tomorrow!"

Another modern objection to speaking of "perfection in love" is our pervasive sense of failure in the Christian life. We feel guilty enough as it is without setting before ourselves a task that can only end in despair. If guilty anger is a part of our negative response to the idea of "perfection in love," however, we are understanding love in legalistic terms. Love is not a duty we grimly perform. It has to do with delight in God and other people even at its hardest. One sixth-century writer who took the suffering of Jesus on the cross very seriously spoke of him being "crucified in the divine cheerfulness." Delight in love is the gift of God, God loving in us. It is not something we can grit our teeth and do, nor is it a possession that, once we have it, makes us good or acceptable. Once we truly understand the connection between love and grace, the wall of legalism that holds us prisoner can be knocked down.

PERFECT LOVE AND CHANGE

The term "perfect" suggests, to us modern people, a state of being which allows for no improvement. We speak of a perfect painting or a perfect circle. We say a day is perfect, or the performance of a piece of music is perfect. In all these we see a quality of completeness. Yet when, except at death, would a person be so complete that we could say "that person is perfect"? People are always changing; that is the basic human condition.

When we give the term "perfection" this meaning, opposing it to change, we are using it as the pagan philosophers did. Heirs of Aristotle and Plato, they believed that human beings cannot be perfect in the way God is perfect precisely because perfection must be unchanging, static, complete. But human beings are always subject to change, and for this reason, compared to God, they are defective—the human habit is to grow from babyhood to adulthood through old age and into death. The very conditions of human life are subject to change, too: the philosophers saw in life nothing but a series of unpredictable ups and downs, and behold, what they saw seemed very bad. "Call no one blessed until that one is dead," warned Herodotus, the Greek historian.

Gregory of Nyssa, a great fourth-century writer on the Christian life, turned this pagan notion upside down. To be a human being, said Gregory, one has to change. It is the way God made us when God set us in creation, for creation itself is always changing. The real issue is not *physical* change at all, but moral or spiritual change, over which we have control. We choose to move toward or away from God. We all belong to two worlds, the world of God in whose image we are created, and the blind, natural world of the animals, which operates according to laws that have little to do with a conscious decision to love. Change has to do with the balance we strike between these two spheres. We become more human by gaining freedom from the enslaving quality of appetites and emotions, more able to love as we move toward God. Understood this way, perfection cannot be unchanging.

Our growing love is a continuous movement into God's love, as the ancient Christian writers say. But because God's love is without limit, and because being human means sharing in the image of God, we can never in our human loving reach the limit of our ability to love. This means that though we may love fully at any one moment, it is not perfect love unless that love continues to grow. "For this is truly perfection: never to stop growing towards what is better and never placing any limit on perfection" (Gr. OP, p. 122). That we can never "arrive," then, is cause for celebration, not despair, because it grows out of our likeness to God.

"PERFECT LOVE" AND BEING A HUMAN BEING

Our ordinary English usage shows us that we do not believe that being human and loving perfectly go together. "I know I forgot to go to the post office to mail the mortgage check; I'm only human!" "How can you expect me to love you with all your flaws? I'm only human!" Notice that by lumping these two statements together we have fallen into the mistake the pagan Greeks made. We are thinking about our physical limitations, over which we have only a little control, in the same terms as we think about our limited but very real control of our temper, the expression of our sexuality, or most important, our love. It is true that, being only human, we are apt to forget things. That we suffer the inconveniences of finiteness no observant person would dispute. But this is a different kind of statement from "I cannot love you with your flaws; I'm only human." In this second statement, "I'm only human" carries with it the implication that we have no more control over our ability to love than we have over our ability to go a month without sleep. It suggests that we believe human beings by their very nature are less than they ought to be but unable to be more than they are. No one feels like this all the time, of course, or bookstores would not be full of self-help books. But this "I'm only human" perspective keeps a lot of people feeling inadequate, guilty, helpless, and angry all at once. How else can we feel if we believe human nature is essentially flawed and cannot change? War is terrible, but human nature is what it is. Exploitation of the poor, minorities, the Third World is awful, but how could it be stopped? No wonder we feel so helpless!

Our early monastic friends could not accept these "truths" of ours. They believed too fervently that, working with the overwhelming gift of God's grace, not only could an individual come to be fully loving in a way that significantly changes the world but also that, in the continuation of the work of God begun in Christ in the incarnation, crucifixion, and resurrection, the whole human race and the cosmos itself would one day be transformed in love.

WHOM DO I LOVE?

If the goal of the Christian life is to love God and our neighbor as ourselves, we still need to ask the question the lawyer asked Jesus: "Yes, but who *is* my neighbor, and what does this have to do with the love of God?" The parable of the Good Samaritan only raises questions: What is Christian "love of myself"? How do love of self, God, and neighbor fit together? Will loving God make me love my neighbor? How do I find my neighbor? How do love of neighbor and my spiritual life go together if care of the neighbor means abandoning my Christian principles?

These were also monastic questions. Dorotheus of Gaza, a sixth-century monk in a highly organized monastery, gives us some of the ancient answers. Dorotheos himself had an intimate and faithful understanding of the principles of the earlier writers, and he is brilliant in his ability to make his points through the use of images, metaphors and parables.

Browsing through his homilies, the reader is struck by how much space Dorotheos gives to the problems of judgmentalism and self-righteousness which must have been common in his monastery. In one homily he exhorts the brothers not to judge or condemn each other, but remember that love of God and of other people are so closely related that it is impossible to love God and have contempt for the sins and weaknesses of other people at the same time. Summing up, he says, "Each one according to his means should take care to be at one with everyone else, for the more one is united to his neighbor, the more he is united with God" (Dor., p. 138). Then he goes on to explain with a wonderful metaphor,

> Suppose we were to take a compass and insert the point and draw the outline of a circle. The center point is the same distance from any point on the circumference. . . . Let us suppose that this circle is the world and that God himself is the center: the straight lines drawn from the circumference to the center are the lives of human beings. . . . Let us assume for the sake of the analogy that to move toward God, then, human beings move from the circumference along the various radii of the circle to the center. But at the same time, the closer they are to God, the closer they become to one another; and the closer they are to one another, the closer they become to God. (Dor., pp. 138–39)

The opposite is also true; as we move away from God we move away from other people, and as we move away from people, we also move away from God.

This is a marvelous metaphor for us moderns, but it is not one that is self-evidently true. It assumes that God is present in a real way in God's own universe, at the center, metaphorically speaking, drawing all people and things to God by a natural love for God, placed in their nature by their creator. It also assumes that all are joined to God as the center of their universe in the same way Gregory of Nyssa meant when he talked about his understanding of perfection above. Gregory had articulated his church's conviction that people decide themselves to move toward God or away from God, to become fully human or less than human. Dorotheus adds to the mix what he claims all the monastic teachers held: that a movement toward God necessarily moves us closer to other people to whom we are joined simply by the way the universe is made.

These are not accepted beliefs in our time. Since the Enlight-
enment it has been more common to understand the universe as
self-contained, with God as a benevolent observer or even absent
altogether. Certainly the expression of and our growth in our individual humanity is not linked with our movement toward God
and other people. Instead, we are accustomed to think of the universe itself as neutral, beautiful, or hostile, depending upon the
circumstances of our thoughts, but we do not see it invested with
the kind of movement toward God that our predecessors saw in
it. Modern science seems to preclude that. As for our responsibility
and love toward other people, we tend to understand it in terms
of universal justice, or we think of it arising out of our own private
religious perceptions that cannot be universalized at all. How can
we make a place for legitimate claims of love in a culture that defines being human in terms of the expression of individuality and
independence over against love?

All these problems together convince many modern Christians
that they could only become real Christians if it were not for the
other people in the world. For them to be Christian means to be
a "spiritual" person, full of love and joy to share with all the human
race, but they find it very hard to be in contact with the real flesh-
and-blood problems of other human beings. In their minds, "spiritual" people "rejoice in the Lord always" and whatever hinders
their rejoicing, including a lot of complexity and ambiguity in life,
gets rejected. Often they can hardly tolerate other people's real
problems or even their personalities. Real people tug them away
from the pure, spiritual love of God.

Related to this rejection of real people is the conviction that the
minister and the church have no business concerning themselves
in social issues. The job of the church and its clergy is to save souls,
not meddle in secular affairs. Christians who believe this do not
believe that God is the metaphorical center of creation, drawing
all things to that center. Instead they place God in another, spiritual
realm, the realm of faith, separate from the flesh-and-blood world
we actually live in. There is a whole generation of schizophrenic
Christians who have two personalities, one for God and the
church, and another for the everyday world of science and common
sense. They do not see the intimate relationship Dorotheos sees
between the love of God and the love of other people.

On the other side of the coin, many people reject Christianity
precisely because they have only known some world-repudiating

version of it, so that they associate being Christian with being in-sensitive to human suffering and need. They often feel that they must choose between loving God and turning their backs on peo-ple, and doing what they can for people while turning their backs on God. But Dorotheos's metaphor suggests that neither the love of God without love of people nor the love of people without the love of God is possible. Human beings are made in the image of God, and this means that we *cannot* love God without at the same time loving God's image.

Furthermore, rather than a growing love of God isolating us from the world and its problems, just the opposite is true—as the saint grew closer to God and to other people, the clearer it became that all people are alike in their sin. The need for self-protection and rejection of other people's sins was gone as the experience of love brought with it confidence in the reality of forgiveness, faith in the mercy of God, and an unwavering hope for transformation. One of the early fathers, Apollo of Scetis, before he took up the monastic life, had murdered a pregnant woman and cut the baby out of her to see what it looked like. Not only was his repentance accepted when he came to join the community; he became one of the great Abbas. Perhaps it is true that only the great lovers of God and other people can look steadily on real human sin and not despair.

THE LOVE OF GOD

We all expect to love our neighbor from the day we become Christian, and we also expect to love God. Unfortunately, our ex-pectations usually have almost nothing to do with what happens. Many of us have no sense of God at all, or if we do, it is more like a sense of duty or even fear toward God. Then, because we believe we should love God, we judge ourselves to be religious failures.

Our ancestors made no such assumptions about Christian love. Gregory of Nyssa, for example, characterized the life of the monk in three stages. At the beginning, she or he serves God out of fear, like a slave; next, the service of God stems from the desire for a reward, like that of a hired hand. Only in the final stage does this person serve God out of friendship with God, or out of the pure love of God, as a child of God's household. The significant point here for us is that the love of God is conceived of as being *difficult*, something to be learned over a very long time. In fact, this is what ascetic discipline was designed to do: to train its practitioners in the ways of God, so that, if God should put that love into their hearts, they might come truly to love God and God's images, other people.

This belief about the relationship between love of God and of humanity and the training for this love was much older than monasticism. It is still one of the most potentially significant lessons the ancient church has to teach us today. If we should come to understand what it was about and believe it as well, our Christianity would be more realistic, and at the same time it would remove from our shoulders a lot of self-condemnation and unwitting hypocrisy.

SELF-LOVE

The issue of self-love and its relation to the other two loves, of God and neighbor, is extremely important. The great Anthony discusses it in a letter he wrote to the male and female monks at Arsinoe in Egypt:

> . . . [The person] who sins against [the neighbor] does evil to [the self]; and [the person] who does good to [the] neighbor does good to [the self]. Otherwise, who is able to do ill to God, or who is there who could hurt [God] . . . or who would ever serve [God] or exalt [God] as [God] deserves? Therefore, while we are still clothed in this heavy body, let us rouse up [the image of] God in ourselves by incitement of each other, and deliver ourselves to death for our souls and for each other; and if we do this, we shall be manifesting the substance of [God's] compassion for us. (Ant., Letter VI, p. 17)

In one sense, the whole of this passage is Anthony's paraphrase of 1 John 4 as he understands it. He begins in this section to state that whatever good or ill we do for another person, we do for ourselves because, as he says elsewhere, we are joined to one another in the body of Christ which is the church.

But he adds another point: while we are able to do good or harm to ourselves and to each other, we cannot directly do anything for God or hurt God. God cannot be insulted or given physical gifts or be directly affected by ordinary modes of human behavior. But human beings are able to affect God by their relationships with other people.

So far we have a pious reason why we are to do good for others. Now Anthony goes on to tie our love for ourselves to the other two loves, of God and of other people. In the same letter he expresses his optimism and gratitude toward God for what he sees God having done for us through the healing of our wounds in Christ. Significantly he goes on to say,

> . . . [God has] gathered us out of all regions, till [God] should make resurrection of our hearts from the earth, and teach us that we are all of one substance and members of one another. Therefore, we ought greatly to love one another. For [one] who loves [one's] neighbor loves God; and [one] who loves God loves [his or her] own soul. (Ant., Letter VI, p. 22)

We ought to love one another, then, for to love the neighbor means to love God, and if we love God, we love ourselves!

But what on earth can this mean? The first part seems clear enough, and is axiomatic in the New Testament. The difficulty in the passage is in equating the love of God with love of ourselves. Nevertheless, Anthony is working out the meaning of Paul's metaphor that the church is the body of Christ, that Christ who is God is its head, and that its members are made up of all of us, so that love of God entails love of the whole of God's body, myself included. Understood in this way this metaphor is worthy of profound meditation.

There is more to it than this, however: a real love for God arises out of the knowledge of what God is like. But at the same time that we begin to have this knowledge, we also come to know what being made in the image of God means. We long to have that image, covered over with the muck of our everyday life, restored to what it was meant to be. Then we are able to begin to seek our own salvation not out of self-hatred, but rather out of a love of our own life. We begin to see that if God loved human beings so much that we were given the gift of the incarnation, the terrible crucifixion, and the resurrection, then no one can offer any Christian justification for despising or hating any human being, ourselves included.

LOVE AS A DISPOSITION

If the love of self, God, and neighbor are so intertwined, the very goal of the Christian life is love. But what is that love? To our monastic ancestors, love can be our goal only in so far as it is a *disposition*, a whole way of being, feeling, seeing and understanding, at which we arrive by a combination of God's grace, our awareness of what we want, and our own choices, which we make every

day of our lives. Love is not a distant point at which we aim with
the expectation that one day we will arrive at it and then live hap-
pily ever after. Instead, love functions as a goal by directing all our
day-to-day actions, even the little ones.

Before further probing the nature of love as a disposition, let us
clear up a difficulty. English has only one term, "love," to describe
two overlapping but very different states which we tend to muddle
together. On the one hand, the word "love" commonly describes
a whole range of emotions that we feel in many different situations,
including "falling in love." Love as an emotion is spontaneous. It
may be more or less intense, and may last only a few minutes or
a reasonably long time. It is a kind of mood that we experience as
coming upon us, bringing with it warm and positive feelings. It
may also be in direct violation of our other principles and values.
This kind of love does not entail action on our part to be real;
though our feelings may push us to act in a certain way, there is
no necessary reason why we have to act on those feelings. (But
see chapter 4, below.)

On the other hand, we use the word "love" in English to mean
a deep attitude of heart, or as a disposition directed at something
or someone with which or with whom we are in a long-term relationship of commitment. Love as we are now speaking of it is
not characterized so much by emotion—though emotion must certainly be part of it—as it is by a commitment we make that shapes
our ways of seeing, understanding, and acting. Where love solely
as an emotion might or might not lead to an appropriate expression
of itself in action, love as a disposition must, by definition, lead to
it. If I love my child, I must not only have warm feelings for her;
I must provide for her to the best of my ability, teach her what I
believe to be good and true, discipline her to learn to care for herself
and others. If I have a bad day and feel hateful to everyone, including her, I do not say "I no longer love you": I try to control
my own feelings and I continue to care for her. Similarly, if I am
a loving spouse, I *feel* love for my husband, but that feeling provides no basis for marriage unless, along with it, is a habitual attitude of heart that wishes for and seeks to provide for his well-
being in concrete acts of kindness, consideration, and service,
every single day, in small ways as well as large ways.

Often, in fact, when we act out of love, what we actually *experience* feels much more like what we ordinarily think of as duty.
But love, as we use it here, includes as part of its very nature a

willingness to care for the other person, which means to take on a real responsibility for another, and in many cases, as every parent knows, a further willingness to sacrifice our own emotional comfort, as we must when we have to say no to something harmful the child really wants.

It is important to note that this kind of love only comes naturally up to a certain point. Past that we have to keep choosing that part of it which seems to run counter to our immediate desires and even needs (one cannot walk out of the house and leave a cranky two-month-old baby alone for three hours no matter how much one needs to!), and often this choosing seems very nearly impossible. Day-to-day love has to be learned and exercised even toward the people we find it easy to love. How much more true it is of the difficult people in our lives we want to love! This kind of love takes practice, a whole lifetime's worth, and it is illustrated in the early monastic life by this whimsical story:

> Going to town one day to sell some small articles, Abba Agathon met a cripple on the roadside, paralysed in his legs, who asked him where he was going. Abba Agathon replied, "To town, to sell some things." The other said, "Do me the favor of carrying me there." So he carried him to the town. The cripple said to him, "Put me down where you sell your wares." He did so. When he had sold an article, the cripple asked, "What did you sell it for?" and he told him the price. The other said, "Buy me a cake," and he bought it.

This questioning and demanding went on for the whole day, presumably, until Agathon was through selling his goods. Then the cripple asked,

> "Do me the favor of carrying me back to the place where you found me." Once more picking him up, he carried him back to that place. Then the cripple said, "Agathon, you are filled with divine blessings, in heaven and on earth." Raising his eyes, Agathon saw [no one]; it was an angel of the Lord, come to try him. (Apoth., Agathon 30, p. 25)

These two kinds of love—emotion, and the long-term attitude of heart which must be learned—seem quite different from each other, but we confuse them, often dangerously, all the time. People get married with sincere feelings of love toward each other and then are bewildered and feel betrayed when they find themselves in marriages in which real demands are put upon them to act upon the love that they feel. Love that is only a good feeling can never be the basis of a happy marriage. This principle applies to our other loves as well: parents love their adorable babies, and then end up in patterns of abuse when their good feelings cannot sustain them through difficult times. Friendships too are made and broken regularly because of the confusion between these two kinds of love.

Now, how is it that love in the sense of emotion could possibly be confused with love as a lived-out commitment? Perhaps it is because we so rarely think of our long-term committed loves as chosen loves. Our love for our children and parents, other family members, and friends to whom we are committed seems to be spontaneous (who could look at their own new baby without being overwhelmed with emotion?) so that we rarely think about the ways in which love of this second kind does not, in fact, perpetuate itself of its own accord.

The distinction between a *temperament* and a *disposition* is instructive at this point. We are more or less born with our temperament, and it persists as we grow up from childhood to adulthood pretty much on its own, though parents, teachers, and friends may try to modify it. The word "temperament" here describes the underlying characteristic and apparently natural attitude a person has toward the world: cheerful, violent, loving, thoughtful, grudging, and so forth. But temperament is not the same as disposition, for "disposition" has to do with a *chosen and cultivated* long-term attitude of heart. Even having a loving temperament is not the same as having a loving disposition, for one can have a loving temperament and still be quite thoughtless, even irresponsible toward others.

Perhaps there is another reason we confuse the two kinds of love. We know quite rightly that, though love has to do with commitment, where there is no long-term loving feeling, there is also no love. Most of us have felt toward someone in our lives a dull sense of duty which we expressed with all the right actions of love while we only felt a deadly indifference or even hostility. There are parents who can hardly bear the sight of their children, yet "do right by them," and there are spouses who behave the same way. We know that this is not love. Even though we cannot *feel* loving all the time, it is clear that there still has to be a continuity between our feelings and our actions toward the significant people in our lives. So, because we know that love as an emotion must, in some way, be a part of love as a disposition, we confuse the two.

The early monastics unanimously believed that, while it is important and difficult to love the people in our lives to whom we are naturally related, including our friends, this is not the full intention of the command of the gospel to love. Rather, we are also to love strangers, people we know to be criminals, the difficult neighbor, people who mock what we stand for, even our enemies. We are to love them, not out of a superior attitude, but with a real love that sees them as human beings, beloved of God, and yet flawed *just as we are ourselves.* And we are to love them, not just at a distance, but up close, as separate individuals, and in concrete ways, involving our actions, as the gospel requires. We are not to say "You fool" to them, or "He does not deserve my care." And certainly, we are not to say, "If I do my duty, pay my taxes, and spend a certain amount of time in good works, I will have fulfilled my obligations of love."

This does not mean that I feel the same toward everyone: we are not asked to enjoy the company of all people equally. Nevertheless, we are commanded to deal with everyone, out of the very disposition of love. And if this is what scripture commands, rather than being perfectly reasonable and sensible, as it was when it described the love of our near and dear, it seems outrageous and impossible. Such love can hardly be human. Can scripture really demand this of us? The early monastics thought it did.

Here it is crucial to remember the difference between love as spontaneous emotion and love as a disposition which comes about as the result of God's grace and our own choices and commitments lived out over a very long period of time. We must not let ourselves for one minute think that Christian love is something that arises in our heart as a gift of God's grace from the moment we become Christian or we set ourselves up for despair or hypocrisy. Love is the *goal* of the Christian life.

But love is not a goal in the same way that the destination of a journey is a goal. I may never fully get to love the way I would when I complete a journey to a geographical location. I would either be there, or I would not, and if I were there, I would have nowhere else to go. Love is a goal in the way being a doctor or a minister or a mother is a goal. If you are a minister, it did not happen all at once with ordination. Rather, ministry is something you came to gradually. You were called to it, you went to seminary, you learned its skills, you came to see as a minister and to make choices as a minister over a very long period of time. You will never be able to say, "Now I am fully a minister; I will never have to give it another thought." The *goal* of ministry, especially if you are already out of school, may rarely arise in your mind as a future goal. Instead, *as a goal* it serves to shape your present, as you make decisions, cultivating in yourself behaviors, attitudes, and habits that help you become more and more what you want to be.

Love is this kind of goal for the teachers of the early church. They wished to come to the point where all their actions, thoughts, and imaginings should be full of love, that they should have the disposition of love, but they spent very little time talking about it. Many of them did not think it was even appropriate to talk about aiming at it. Instead, they used their reflection upon that ultimate goal, love, to enable themselves to set priorities and make decisions in their everyday dealings with other people.

Here is a story told of a monk of the first generation who had been made bishop and found himself having to deal with an illegitimately pregnant girl:

> [Father] Ammonas advanced to the point where his goodness was so great, he took no notice of wickedness. Thus, having become bishop, someone brought a young girl who was pregnant to him, saying, "See what this unhappy wretch has done; give her a penance." But he, having marked the young girl's womb with the sign of the cross, commanded that six pairs of fine linen sheets should be given to her, saying, "It is for fear that, when she comes to give birth, she may die, she or the child, and have nothing for her burial." But her accusers resumed, "Why did you do that? Give her a punishment." But he said to them, "Look, brothers, she is near death; what am I to do?" Then he sent her away and no old man dared accuse anyone anymore. (Apoth., Ammonas 8, p. 27)

The bishop's followers expected him to execute God's justice: he was the representative of the church, she had sinned, and he must decide her punishment. If his own goal was a union with God that excluded any real concern for others, he would have sent her to someone else. But his goal was love; his treatment of her must nourish this love. And so he looked at her and saw a young girl, maybe no more than thirteen, probably abandoned by her family and the good church people who desired to uphold the law of God. She was in danger of death in childbirth and perhaps so poor that she could not even have a decent burial. And so he gave her the sheets.

Love as a disposition does not primarily act on abstract principle. Instead it is a way of seeing habitually and responding to the real, separate, individual needs of each of the people we encounter in our lives every single day.

GRACE AND HUMAN EFFORT

Loving can be a difficult business. It is impossible to grit the teeth and love, no matter how much we want to. That is because human effort is only one of the two basic elements necessary for the fulfillment of all Christian goals and desires, but particularly for love. The other is God's grace. Without grace, nothing is possible. The way these two come together is so important in the theology of the early church that there is a special term, "synergism" ("working with"), to describe it.

The third-century writer Origen of Alexandria explains the relationship between our effort and God's grace with a metaphor: It is like traveling in a sailing ship on the ocean. Our life is like the ship, and we are the captain. All our skill, energy, and attention are necessary to avoid shipwreck and arrive in port, for the ocean is dangerous and inattention is disastrous upon it. Our ship, however, also needs the wind. It is the wind that fills the sails and moves the ship, and when the two are weighed against each other, the skill of the captain seems very small compared with the contribution of the wind. In Origen's metaphor the wind represents God's help and grace. Great as that grace is, the human being must work, with all the skill and energy he or she can muster, in order to love.

In the same way, it is truly God who saves us; it is not something we can do on our own. Not for one minute did the early theologians and monastics of our Christian heritage think otherwise. But a ship cannot sail itself, and the wind will not take matters into its own hands (so to speak!) to sail the ship without the attention and work of the human sailor. To use an example, praying to God to make us love without any other effort on our part will not make us love. God's grace is more like wind in a sail than it is like lightning. God will not change our hearts without a real participation on our parts.

There are many examples of this early monastic understanding of the relationship between grace and human effort in the literature, but there is a good, blunt example in the sayings attributed to Anthony. Presumably, the brother in the story had come to Anthony for counsel in a difficult matter involving a temptation or a habit that he could not control, and he asked for Anthony's prayers.

> A brother said to Abba Anthony, "Pray for me." The old man said to him, "I will have no mercy upon you, nor will God have any, if you yourself do not make an effort and if you do not pray to God." (Apoth., Anthony 16, p. 4)

"No, I will not pray for you," we hear Anthony reply to his request. "If you yourself do not try to master your own problem and pray about it as you do, my prayers will do you no good, and as for God's help, God will not let you off the hook without your own deliberate and hard-working cooperation."

But how does this work? and what human effort are we to make? Sometimes, though we do not know exactly how God's grace will come to us, we know what we desire for ourselves. Knowing this much as Christians is important. As Anthony said,

> . . . Whoever hammers a lump of iron, first decides what he is going to make of it, a scythe, a sword, or an axe. Even so we ought to make up our minds what kind of virtue we want to forge or we labor in vain. (Apoth., Anthony 35, p. 8)

To choose the tool we are to make, we must not simply aim at love in general; we must have a little knowledge of the qualities that lead to the love we want: perhaps patience, or an ability to listen. In the same way, we must also know what we are to avoid: grudge-holding or gossiping. There are times when all of this seems very obvious and easy to know.

But sometimes we are so mired in the world we live in, with its temptations, habits, and ways of seeing and feeling, that we do not even know what is wrong with us; we only know that something is wrong, and we feel helpless. In this case, says one of the fathers, our human effort may be tiny, but it is still of crucial importance. It consists in calling out to God for help, simply *saying* "God help me." This much we can always do. The early monastics were more aware than we of the way obsessive emotional and social situations often act to take away almost all human freedom, but they insisted we can always call for help. Growing up in a bad family or neighborhood environment, being deprived of basic necessities, cannot keep a person from God. Furthermore, as Dorotheos of Gaza said, God pities the struggling; therefore, God probably looks with more compassion at a murderer who has struggled against his or her temptation and lost than on a monk who is thoughtless.

SOURCES OF GRACE

How do we experience this grace? It is not a kind of spiritual lightning bolt that hits us out of the blue, whether we ask for it or not. Not that God never works that way. But God does not relate to human beings as a watchmaker adjusting a watch; that would violate the human freedom that belongs to the image of God in which we were made. God will never answer the prayer "please God, make me love" if we simply pray it over and over.

Furthermore, grace is not a religious experience we wait for. The early monastics were distrustful of religious experiences because of the human ability to make subjective needs and desires into truths about the universe. They were extraordinarily aware of the way religious experiences could claim for themselves a significance in our lives that even we, with our modern way of conceptualizing, would have to characterize as diabolical. Think, for example, of the sort of story we hear regularly about someone who thought he or she had received a message from God to go and kill a particular person or group of people. But the monastics were also talking about the much more common situation where a religious experience is so vivid that the whole of the rest of the Christian life, including the shared witness and fellowship of other Christians, is set aside as false.

This does not mean, of course, that the early monastics discounted religious experience altogether, but they did not believe one should seek it as a source of grace. If one had it, it had to be tested against the revelation of God in scripture, in Christ, and in the community of fellow Christians in the church. One should never confuse its value with the Christian goal of love of God and of God's image, other people.

Though they never say it in quite these words, what grace is, as they understood it, is simply God's help in seeing and knowing the world, ourselves, God, and other people in such a way that love is made possible.

They expected this grace first of all in the sacraments, in baptism, then in the Eucharist, the Lord's Supper. They knew that they were the body of Christ, and that God had promised grace when Christians gather for that meal as Christ's body with Christ among them as their head.

They also looked for grace in and through prayer. Though there was a wide variety of ways of praying among these early fathers and mothers, from reciting the psalms to wordless meditation, there was agreement on two points: that one *must* pray and that prayer was a source of grace. We will discuss how this can happen in chapter 5.

A third source of grace along with the sacraments and prayer for these early monastics was other people. Foremost were the teachers, the Abbas and Ammas of their own small or large communities, who held their position by virtue of their own ability to teach by example and word. To these Abbas and Ammas the brothers and sisters told the innermost secrets of their struggles with their Christian discipline, and in return their teachers looked into their hearts and "gave them a word" in the form of insight, practical suggestions, exercises, and stories and sayings like the ones that appear in this book. In this way they really lived out part of the expectation that they be Christ to each other. We are fortunate if we have friends to act informally in this role for us.

But they also expected all sorts of people to be real sources of grace, too. There are touching stories of monks (unfortunately women would never have been encouraged to encounter a wide range of people) learning important lessons even from pagan priests. As for us, we often miss such opportunities because we dismiss quickly people who are not like us, or who make us socially uncomfortable.

To give a simple example: there are many generous people in the world who, nevertheless, find it hard to receive from others. A friend told me once of an incident in which he had tried to express gratitude to someone who had been enormously helpful to him by paying for his help. But the one who had been helpful knew his friend very well, and he confronted him on his inability to receive without feeling it as a debt to be squared as quickly as possible. And he told my friend that he would not understand the gospel until he learned that its very essence was that grace in all its forms had to be received without payment of any sort. This confrontation brought my friend up short and opened his eyes so that he was able to see that, yes, he *was* unable to receive and it was causing him and others serious pain, as he conceived of love as something he wished to give, but not something he wished to receive because it made him feel "beholden." He had never quite realized this before. Immediately he began to work hard at learning to accept things from other people with gratitude, and it became a kind of turning point in his life. He began to learn what Dorotheos stresses, that nothing we receive is earned; even our ability to do good is a gift of God to be received with gratitude.

This is a good example of the way grace comes to us significantly and unexpectedly from other people, and at the same time, it well illustrates how synergism works: my friend could have simply grown angry and embarrassed at being confronted and shrugged the whole thing off, and if this had happened, though he would have been offered grace, it would have had no effect on him. But he recognized it for what it was and responded with his own work of thought, and repentance, and then gratitude, and as a result, though he has to remember his lesson occasionally, he sees the world, God, himself, and other people in a different light.

In the whole of the Christian life, grace does not come just once to open our eyes, however. It comes again and again as we continue to respond to it and act upon it so that there is a kind of circle or spiral of synergism, as grace and human effort come together leading us deeper into love, farther into the restoration of the image of God. Let me give another modern example. A woman I know had had great difficulties in her relationship with her mother over the years; her mother had seemed to her to be harsh and critical and unloving, though she had wanted her love very badly, and she struggled hard and vainly not to be afraid of her even in her adult years. Then, when she was well past thirty-five she met someone who had known her mother as a child, and who told her things about the unhappiness of her mother's childhood she had never even suspected. Suddenly she found herself overwhelmed with an entirely new desire to protect her mother and care for her. Her heart had been freed to see her mother not as the one who had a mother's power over her but as a person who was herself in need of gentleness and attention. As she understood this, she was given further insights into her mother over a long period of time, and to each of them she continued to respond and grow in love. She found that once she had begun to be attentive to her mother's needs, her mother, too, became a continuing source of grace for her as her anxiety and mistrust of others receded.

Notice, in this example, how when grace first came my friend had a choice: she could have angrily refused to let what she heard about her mother's childhood touch her. In this case, though grace would have been offered, it would have been rejected: what happened to her depended on her positive response. Further, grace did not come just once; after she received it, she was able to see what she had not seen before, and this laid her open to see more and more, and thus to love more and more, as grace was offered, accepted, offered, and accepted. This is the way grace works. "To every one who has will more be given, and he [she] will have abundance; but from him [her] who has not, even what he [she] has will be taken away" (Matt. 25:29). The receiving of grace is never automatic; it depends upon a constant attentiveness and willingness to listen and to look. This is what Poemen means when he says, " . . . If Moses had not led his sheep to Midian he would not have seen him who was in the bush" (Apoth., Poemen 195, p. 194).

Grace belongs fully and wholly to the human realm of love as well as the divine. Though there are private aspects to it, it is not finally private, because it is not a matter only between the soul and God. Grace may be viewed with the help of Dorotheos's example of the circle: the closer we move to God the closer we move to each other.

Chapter 3

Humility

Love is the goal of the Christian life: love of God and neighbor. Most of human life as the early monastics experienced it, however, left little place for love. Their culture, as is ours, was characterized by a continual jostling for power and a need to dominate others. Short-term gratification took the place of concern for the long-term well-being of others. In the place of love they saw the ever-present need to be right all the time, and the struggle to feed those appetites that only seem to grow greater as they are satisfied—appetites for money, possessions, prestige, food. They saw that all of these, in some way or another, came out of the hides of their neighbors, especially the poor.

The pile of problems that stood in the way of love were so enormous that no one could expect to continue to live by these standards of the world and to love. According to the monastics, it was possible to live "in the world" with family, property, and career and be Christian if certain basic internal attitudes and ways of looking at things were renounced and others cultivated in their place. Those who chose the monastic life, however, believed that for themselves only radical renunciation of the external as well as the internal patterns of their culture could put them in a position where they would be able to begin to love. This was why they did what may seem so self-destructive to us in the present: they sold their property, refused marriage, gave up careers, and turned their backs on everything their culture valued. It was not necessarily that these things were evil—marriage, for example, is never portrayed as evil. They were seen, however, to be a constant source of self-deception and temptation. We will discuss what these temp-

tations were, whether they were real, and how we might suc-
cessfully face the significant ones without choosing such a radical
option of total renunciation in the next chapters.

In any event, physically fleeing the everyday world was only
the exterior beginning of the monastic life. The interior beginning
of the process of growth in love, more fundamental than any material renunciation, was the cultivation of a deep Christian attitude
of heart that could make love possible. Their name for this attitude
was humility.

> When Abba Macarius was returning from the marsh to his cell one
> day carrying some palm-leaves, he met the devil on the road with
> a scythe. The [devil] struck at him as much as he pleased, but in
> vain, and he said to him, "What is your power, Macarius, that makes
> me powerless against you? All that you do, I do, too; you fast, so
> do I; you keep vigil, and I do not sleep at all; in one thing only do
> you beat me." Abba Macarius asked what that was. He said, "Your
> humility. Because of that I can do nothing against you." (Apoth.,
> Macarius 11, p. 130)

If this was true for Macarius, it was also true for any other person
who wished to be a Christian. Anyone can fast or renounce what
they love in order to gain what they want more. The devil himself
is good at renunciation; there is no merit in that. For these early
folk, the mark of the Christian was not renunciation or, for that
matter, heroic feats of virtue, but humility.

> Abba Anthony said, "I saw all the snares that the enemy spreads
> out over the world, and I said, groaning, 'What can get me through
> such snares?' Then I heard a voice saying to me, 'Humility.'"
> (Apoth., Anthony 7, p. 2)

It was humility that made these ancient Christians able with the
help of God's grace to take on the enormous and dangerous task
of the transformation of the old creation into the new.

But what was this humility, this world-transforming attitude of
heart, that made this possible? Most basically, it was the living-
out of the conviction that all human beings, every man, woman,
and child, are beloved creatures of God.

Human beings are creatures. We are limited by our physical conditions, our emotional needs, and our proneness to sin. As *God's*
creatures, though, we are each one loved by God in our frailty,
sin, and all. These early monastics put at the very heart of their
understanding of what it means to be Christian the fundamental
biblical message we find in so many forms: "while we were yet

sinners Christ died for us" (Rom. 5:8). It is the sick who need the physician, not the well.

This basic attitude of humility recognizes that no person loves or does any good without the help of God, so that whatever acts of kindness or virtue a person performs, whatever strength or happiness one has, one's ability to work well and to love well—all these are possible because God gives them to the creatures as God's good gifts. No one is in a position to look down on another from a superior height because of her or his hard work or piety or mental superiority. We are all vulnerable, all limited, and we each have a different struggle only God is in a position to judge.

Out of such a fundamental attitude of heart for the women and men of the desert could flow a whole way of Christian living, and, paradoxically, humility could become not only the attitude out of which this way of life would come but also the means by which such living might become possible.

OVERCOMING FALSE VIEWS OF HUMILITY

Before we can look more closely at the content of humility, however, we need to talk about some special problems the very word "humility" raises in our modern context. We do not use the word "humility" in our modern world in the same way ancient Christians did, and if we try to substitute our modern meanings where the ancient word appears, the literature will not only fail to be helpful, it will be repulsive, especially to women and minorities who have had to struggle for their own self-esteem as well as their place in the world and even in the church.

The meaning of the word as it was used in these early monastic writers seems to have been lost fairly early. Across the many centuries of the Christian era up to the modern world when women have been exhorted to be humble, humility included as one of its components being obedient to their husbands, fathers, brothers, and/or priests. Humility has been a shorthand word for recognizing and accepting an inferior position in the world. Sometimes it has included accepting that other people had a right to buy or sell them.

At various times women have accepted that only their role, not that of men, is service, that they must sacrifice their lives, desires, feelings, and needs for the sake of those of their families, that they must give up their selves for the sake of others to whom they belong. Abused women have been told by their pastors that their men would not abuse them if they did not provoke it. Wives are still told that marriage is mainly the work of women.

The real difficulty is not so much that women have been taught to serve but that service seems to demand loss of self. The very phrase "selfless love" raises a specter of a woman without any needs, desires, or even personality of her own.

Furthermore, not only women have been hurt by such an equation of service and what is really false humility. One of the significant contributions of the women's movement is the way it has become apparent that men too have been hurt by this imbalance. In twentieth-century American culture, very few women or men are lucky enough not to have to struggle out of some form of this mind-set, no matter how well educated or independent they may be. So, love of God and neighbor means in a significant way that we cannot be "selfless" in the way we usually mean it. None of this mind-set of "selflessness" has to do with humility as we meet it in our texts. Remember Anthony's letter? He says "[one] who loves [one's] neighbor loves God; and [one] who loves God loves [his or her] own soul" (Ant., Letter VI, p. 22).

Though certain statements taken out of context might make us think so, humility has nothing to do with a low self-image. As we saw in chapter 2, God's love for us and the presence of God's image in each of us means that we are to love ourselves and value ourselves as well as others. Women placing a low value on the self, and living only to serve others, has far more to do with the economic conditions and conveniences of our—and their—culture than it has to do with God.

Christian women not only have no obligation to place such a low value on themselves, they must not. How can a Christian woman's family be her "whole life"? A Christian's primary loyalty and love belong to God, who has given each of us our life. A Christian may not give her or his life to another person as that person's absolute center. Such devotion properly belongs to God alone.

Besides, it is only a real love of God that makes life-giving love of service possible. Humility in the ancient texts nearly always has to do with relationships, but it works to set the woman or man who embodies it free to escape ordinary internal cultural patterns of dominance and subservience. One reason the monastics left ordinary life in their own culture was that they were trying to establish a new model where everyone was on the same footing, where loving service was the model for everybody.

It is not only women who have trouble with the term "humility" in a modern context, however. For many people, it is almost a synonym for manipulative self-sacrifice. The presumably humble statement "you take the only good chair" carries the unspoken message "and then you will be in my debt so that I can ask something of you later." What is produced in the person who accepts its conditions is guilt and resentment. Unfortunately, so many of us have been so victimized by this pattern of relating to people at home, in church, and at work that both the words "self-sacrifice" and "humility" fill us with horror. One result is that to talk with any meaning of the humility or self-sacrifice of Christ has become nearly impossible to a good many people. But the "you take the only good chair" way of dealing with others is manipulation, not humility. It is a gross perversion of Christianity, and it needs to be recognized for what it is. Real humility brings freedom and love to its recipients, not guilt and resentment.

In a related manner, we often believe that "feeling guilty" is associated with humility. But feeling guilty—as opposed to recognizing actual guilt, repenting, and moving forward—has nothing to do with humility either. We often make a virtue out of continuing to feel guilty about something we have done or failed to do, believing at some level that this paralyzing feeling is a kind of penance we ought to do. We associate feeling guilty with deliberately taking on ourselves a low self-esteem, and this destructive state of mind often produces inaction.

Real humility, however, mobilizes, it does not immobilize. "A brother questioned Abba Poemen saying, 'What does it mean to repent of a fault?' The old man said, 'Not to commit it again in the future" (Apoth., Poemen 120, p. 184). Humility *accepts* our human vulnerability and the fact that we sin. It is not so overwhelmed by human weakness that it is left paralyzed, thinking over its own inadequacy. One of the Sayings of the Fathers expresses it tersely in this way: An Abba asked Anthony what special word of advice he had to help him in his life. Anthony replied, "Do not trust in your own righteousness. Do not worry about [sin that is] past . . ." (Apoth., Anthony 6, p. 2). A longer saying includes an explicit exchange on the subject of feeling guilty.

A brother said to Abba Poemon, "If I fall into a shameful sin, my conscience devours and accuses me saying: 'Why have you fallen?'" The old man said to him, "At the moment when a [person] goes astray, if [that person] says, I have sinned, immediately the sin ceases." (Apoth., Poemen 99, p. 181)

Feeling guilty has nothing to do with humility, for both real humility and repentance do not paralyze but rather free us up to keep on going.

GIVING UP THE HEROIC SELF-IMAGE

Refusing to wallow in guilt brings us right up to a discussion of the content of humility, how it actually functions for the ancient Christian woman or man, and how it might function for us in our Christian lives.

To begin with, nobody took up the life of the nun or monk without knowing that such a life would entail a lifelong process of inner discipline, prayer, and work. One could not expect to love God and the neighbor as the self the first day out in the desert—no one believed this love would follow immediately or automatically upon renunciation of the world. Nevertheless, it was an enormous temptation to the beginner to see herself or himself as a hero, confronted with heroic-sized tasks to perform in order to reach that goal of love. Unfortunately, being human, and suffering from human frailty, that same beginner would eventually fail; she would pick a fight with a sister, fall asleep during an all-night vigil, eat during a fast. Perhaps a male monk might even follow a girl home from the market. Then would come the inevitable, soul-destroying despair.

It was a temptation to think even of prayer itself in terms of heroic-sized tasks that must be performed. *The Life of St. Anthony* includes a statement that the beginner may sometimes feel that everytime he or she lies down to sleep he or she ought to get up and pray. Anthony warns his followers that these very strong urges to pray are demonic in origin, and the demons urge people on "not for the sake of piety or truth, but so that they might bring the simple to despair, and declare the discipline useless . . . " (V.A. 25, p. 50) as the overconscientious soul was worn out by the attempt to do what is humanly impossible. It is probably a rare Christian today who has not experienced the same urge in a much milder form to read scripture, or pray, or whatever, a certain length of time every day and gave up the attempt in despair after a few days or weeks. That demoralized Christian had simply decided one *ought* to be able to spend an hour a day at some Christian discipline without considering his or her own limitations and setting the task at a manageable size to begin with.

Beginners in the desert had to learn to be humble, that is, to abandon the heroic image of the self and learn to believe that all human beings, themselves included, were weak and vulnerable. They needed to learn instead to take up appropriate tasks, and appropriate tasks for weak and vulnerable human beings are ones that can actually be performed. They had to learn to accept it as true that all tasks contribute to the final goal, and the small ones are often of infinite significance. Someone asked Abba Poemen what it means to lay down your life for your neighbor: Abba Poemen answered,

> . . . When a [person] hears a complaining word and struggles against himself [or herself], and does not . . . begin to complain; when a [person] bears an injury with patience, and does not look for revenge; that is when a [person] lays down his [or her] life for his [or her] neighbor. (Say., p. 183)

How much easier it is to daydream about the dramatic acts of love and self-sacrifice I or the church might make to prove our love of God or neighbor! But the temptation to regard such small actions as unimportant while there are so many serious social problems in the world is the temptation to understand the Christian life only in heroic proportions.

Dorotheos of Gaza, whom we have already met, would suggest to us that the "large" tasks are only accomplished by seeing the way the small lead to and enable the large:

> Suppose there are two ladders, one going upwards to heaven, and the other leading down to hell. You are standing on the earth between the two ladders. You would not reason it all out and say, "How can I fly from the earth and be once and for all on the top of the ladder?" This is impossible and God does not ask it of us, but he does ask that we meanwhile keep from going downwards, and do not harm our neighbor nor offend him . . . nor demean him. And so at last we begin to do a little good and are of help to him in speech, and bear with him, and if he needs something give it [to] him freely, so we go up one rung at a time until finally, with God's help, we reach the top of the ladder. For through this repeated coming to your neighbor's rescue, you come to long for what is advantageous for him as well as advantageous for yourself. This is "love your neighbor as yourself." If we seek, we shall find: and if we ask God, he will enlighten us. (Dor., pp. 206–7)

If we wish to love our neighbor, we start small by trying first to avoid harming the neighbor, refusing to gossip about the neighbor, and offering small help. But if we remember the goal of love and work at it, God will help in the day-to-day struggle, and finally will grant the love we seek—but not as a reward for heroic effort or virtue.

Individuals and churches need to benefit from this advice from the ancient church. Often we Christians individually and collectively fail to take any responsibility for relieving social evils like poverty, hunger, war, or racism because we think so much in terms of the enormity of the task and the smallness of anything we could appear to do to relieve it. What is one blanket contributed to a night shelter if a hundred are needed? How can putting ten homeless people in the church basement on cold nights make any difference compared to the need—especially when the church down the street is putting up fifty? That we even fall into this temptation to substitute thinking big for looking for the small steps we can actually perform is itself the result of forgetting the goal of the Christian life, which is to love God and neighbor—the specific, particular individual neighbor in need, as well as whole groups of neighbors whom we have never met.

GIVING UP THE NEED TO BE
ABOVE REPROACH

Part of the process of giving up the heroic was learning to let go of the feeling that, unless one's actions could be totally free of self-interest, there was no point in doing them because they would be tainted. But to worry about one's purity of motive, said the teachers to their students, was to confuse the means, that is, a life of Christian discipline, with the end, the life of love:

> A brother said to Abba Poemen, "If I give my brother a little bread or something else, the demons tarnish these gifts, saying it was only done out of a desire for praise." The old man said to him, "Even if it is out of desire for praise, we must give the brother what he needs." He told the following parable: "Two farmers lived in the same town; one of them sowed and reaped a small and poor crop, while the other, who did not even trouble to sow reaped absolutely nothing. If a famine comes upon them, which of the two will find something to live on?" The brother replied, "The one who reaped the small poor crop." The old man said to him, "So it is for us; we sow a little poor grain, so that we will not die of hunger." (Apoth., Poemen 51, pp. 173–74)

Humility   49

Whether I give grudgingly or gladly, out of desire to be recognized or hoping not to be recognized, has little to do with the neighbor's *need* that must be fulfilled. Love does not center on itself: "I was hungry and you gave me food," Jesus says in Matt. 25:35, and he says nothing about the state of mind of the giver. Not that the state of mind does not matter, it is just that filling the need of the neighbor comes before questions about the purity of our motives when we do it.

A humble heart remembers that to remain above reproach is not the fundamental task of the Christian. Some of the stories illustrating this point are very funny; one brother, for example, regarded as too rigid by his teacher, is set to stealing from the other monks by his Abba, who afterward stealthily returns what he has stolen in the middle of the night.

Some of the stories are shocking to us—as they would have been to our own ancient counterparts:

> Abba Alonius said to Abba Agathon: "Suppose two men committed murder in your presence and one of them fled to your cell. When the police, coming in search of him, ask you, 'Is the murderer with you?' unless you lie, you hand him over to execution." (Apoth., Alonius 4, p. 35)

The point of this story is not to say that murder is unimportant, for it certainly is. Its true meaning is illustrated by another saying that we meet in Isaac of Nineveh, a later writer well steeped in this tradition, that God's justice compared with God's mercy is like a grain of sand balanced against a load of gold: even God's justice takes second place to God's own love for God's creatures. How often do we injure another person in small or great ways because, remembering that it is important to be truthful, we forget that truthfulness is only a virtue on the road to love, not an end in itself?

It is not that "the means justifies the end" or that morality is purely a matter of relativity. This remembering the purpose of the law—to serve love—is set firmly in a context of certain sins the monastic must not commit, including actions ranging from adultery to gossiping. Nevertheless, there is another whole category of actions that we perform or avoid not as ends in themselves, but rather to move us toward our goal of love. Fasting and living in solitude are examples from the ancient texts.

But there is a third category of actions which under some circumstances are grave sins, and under others are minor compared with the greater harm we would do by failing to commit them.

Under certain circumstances perhaps they are not even sins at all. If the fulfillment of the moral law for its own sake is seen to be the point of the law, the temptation is, in cases of doubt, to err on the side of caution. But if the point of the law is love, then the Christian must be prepared to take real risks for the sake of other people. A failure to lie in the story above would be tantamount to passing a death sentence on the murderer, and thus would be usurping what only God is qualified to do as well as making repentance impossible to the murderer once executed. But the lie in this story could also have had serious consequences. Suppose the monk was himself thrown in jail as an accessory? Suppose the murderer murdered others? It must have been a great temptation to the early Christian monastic to try to codify the moral law for himself or herself in such a way that there would be no ambiguity left, that one could always know what to do without having to take responsibility for the suffering of others that might result from one's moral action. Unfortunately, there was no way to avoid having to use one's own judgment then, just as there is no way now, once it is granted that the goal is love rather than fulfilling a legal code.

Somehow, the very idea that we should at all times be above reproach makes a mockery of repentance and forgiveness as well as of love. It suggests the need always to look good in the sight of the neighbor, never to be caught at fault. We will return to this very familiar desire always to be right more than once in the following pages.

THE IMPORTANCE OF REPENTANCE
AND FORGIVENESS

Perhaps one of the hardest things about living with the uncertainty of the outcome of some of our toughest decisions is that we do not believe in the possibility of forgiveness for our mistakes. We find it hard to admit them in the first place and we have so much trouble distinguishing between "feeling guilty" and acknowledging guilt for the purpose of forgiveness that we are left unable to ask for it. This is the unwelcome heritage of many of us who grew up groveling in a religion that seemed to demand that we continually acknowledge our total unworthiness and repulsive helplessness before God.

Confession of guilt was something quite different to our monastic ancestors. It was a freeing experience that cut them loose from the weight of the past in order to be able to begin each day as the start of a new unburdened life. Humility made it easy to repent or confess to wrongdoing and accept forgiveness, because the humble person knew very well that not only are all human beings sinners—himself or herself included—humility has no problem believing that God loves us and will not reject us, even damaged by sin:

> A soldier asked Abba Mius if God accepted repentance. After the old man had taught him many things he said, "Tell me my dear [friend], if your cloak is torn, do you throw it away?" He replied, "No, I mend it and use it again." The old man said to him, "If you are so careful about your cloak, will not God be equally careful of his creatures?" (Apoth., Mius 3, p. 150)

Perhaps this is close to what Jesus intended when he said that God knows when each sparrow falls and the number of hairs on each of our heads; creation is too precious to God to be discarded just because it is flawed.

Humility has no self-image to maintain. It does not, out of embarrassment, hide its sins from itself or others. It knows already that human beings are prone to sin, and it is ever watchful to escape it. But when sin occurred for the ancient monastic, there was, theoretically at least, no temptation to deny it, no temptation to beat the breast and say, "How could I have done such a thing?" The answer was well known already. "I did it because I, too, am a creature, subject to sin. I was not watchful enough." Pervasive guilt, self-loathing, despair over a committed sin, these were not problems to those able to confess, repent, and receive forgiveness. As Poemen explained it to a brother who told him, "'If I fall into a shameful sin my conscience devours me . . . , ' 'At the moment a person goes astray, if that person says, "I have sinned," immediately the sin ceases'" (Apoth., Poemen 99, p. 181).

Furthermore, even if that person were blamed for a sin actually committed by someone else, there was no self-righteous anger. Rather, it was accepted as fact that there had been other, real sins actually committed for which the man or woman had never had to pay. If one could not repent of the sin for which one was accused, one could always repent of others, and thus go on one's way with cheerfulness. Dorotheos asks his readers,

> Now do you perceive the power of lowliness? . . . In point of fact, there is nothing more powerful than lowliness. If a painful experience comes to a humble man, straightway he goes against himself,

straightway he accuses himself as the one worthy of punishment, and he does not set about accusing anyone or putting the blame on anyone else. For the rest, he goes on his way untroubled, unde-pressed, in complete peace of mind. (Dor., p. 96)

THE STRUGGLE TO AVOID BEING JUDGMENTAL

The recognition of one's own proneness to sin was a powerful component in the humility of the desert fathers and mothers. It also provided the major weapon in their arsenal against the most dangerous temptation they could commit in a way of life that took as its goal the love of neighbor as the self—the temptation to pass judgment on the actions and life of the neighbor. Very nearly the hardest temptation we struggle against, says Dorotheos, is judging our neighbor:

> That Pharisee who was praying and giving thanks to God for [his own] good works was not lying but speaking the truth, and he was not condemned for that. For we *must* give thanks to God when we are worthy to do something good, as he is then working with us and helping us. Because of this he was not condemned, as I said, not even because he said, "I am not like other men," but . . . because he said, "I am not like this tax-collector." It was then that he made a judgment. He condemned a person and the disposition of his soul—to put it shortly, his whole life. Therefore the tax-collector, rather than the Pharisee went away justified. (Dor., p. 132)

The Pharisee went away unjustified, not because he was pleased with his righteousness, but rather because he looked with con-tempt upon a particular tax collector's very being because of his sin. The Pharisee in this story would have been peculiarly repre-sentative of the brother or sister, whose life was meant to be char-acterized by its strict discipline.

> Everyone of us is very careful, on every occasion, to throw the blame on his brother and to strike him down with its weight. Every one of us is negligent and keeps none of the commandments, and we demand in return that our neighbors keep them all. (Dor., p. 144)

But the Gospel was clear:

> Abba Theodore said . . . "Do not judge the fornicator, for you your-self would then transgress the law just as much yourself. He who said 'do not fornicate' also said, 'do not judge.'" (Apoth., Theodore of Eleutheropolis 3, p. 80)

No one can judge another, for no one but God knows why or

how people come to act as they do. What comes easily to one comes with difficulty to another, and only God can weigh all things, even in such a case as that of a mass murderer.

> [One] person can know nothing of the judgments of God [concerning another person]. How do you know how much and how well he fought against it, how much blood he sweated before he did it? Perhaps so little fault can be found in him that God can look on his action as if it were just, for God looks on his labor and all the struggle he had before he did it, and has pity on him. . . . You may well know about the sin, but you do not know about the repentance. (Dor., p. 135)

To be humble is to identify with the sinner, and rather than take secret pleasure in another person's downfall, when you hear of it, say, "Oh Lord, him today, me tomorrow!" recognizing your kinship with the sinner. Here is the way an ancient priest learned this hard lesson:

> A priest of Pelusia heard it said of some brethren that they often went to the city, took baths, [and did not act like monks]. He went to [their worship service] and took [their monastic clothes] away from them. Afterwards, his heart was moved, he repented and went to see Abba Poemen, obsessed by his thoughts. He brought the monastic habits of the brothers and told him all about it. The old man said to him, "Don't you sometimes have something of the old Adam in you?" The priest said, "I have my share of the old Adam." The Abba said to him, "Look, you are just like the brethren yourself; if you have even a little share of the old Adam, then you are subject to sin in the same way." So the priest went and called the brothers and asked their pardon. . . . (Apoth., Poemen 11, p. 168)

All of us have some of the old Adam or Eve in us and so none of us is in a position to judge someone else self-righteously.

But humility went even further than this: one must not simply refuse to judge another; one must also protect the sinner from the consequences of the sin. This is because there is a real expectation that such radical acts of love will have a transforming effect on the heart of the sinner. Here is one funny story among a large number making this point in the Sayings of the Fathers:

> Abba Ammonas came one day to eat in a place where there was a monk of evil repute. Now it happened that a woman came and entered the cell of the brother of evil reputation. The dwellers of that place, having learned this, were troubled and gathered together to chase the brother from his cell. Knowing that Bishop Ammonas was in the place, they asked him to join them. When the brother in question learned this, he hid the woman in a large cask. The crowd of

monks came to the place. Now Abba Ammonas saw the position clearly, but for the sake of God he kept the secret; he entered, seated himself on the cask, and when they had searched everywhere without finding the woman, Abba Ammonas said, "What is this? May God forgive you for this accusation!" After praying he made everyone go out, then taking the brother by the hand he said, "Brother, be on your guard." With these words, he withdrew. (Apoth., Ammonas 10, p. 28)

Abba Poemen was asked, "If I see my brother committing a sin, is it right to conceal it?" Poemen answered, "At the very moment when we hide our brother's fault, God hides our own, and at the moment when we reveal our brother's fault, God reveals ours, too" (Apoth., Poemen 64, p. 175).

HUMILITY AND CHRISTIAN POWER

Humility as the early monastics describe it has nothing to do with passivity, nor anything to do with deliberately cultivating a poor self-image. Being a doormat is not being humble, nor is giving up the self in order to serve the needs, desires, and whims of another person who is not God. Humility is not sniveling, nor is it daydreaming gentle thoughts while the world's violence goes on around it.

Humility is difficult. Much of what is depicted in the literature seems nearly impossible to carry out and it certainly is without the grace of God's help. Humility itself is countercultural, as it was in the fourth, fifth, and sixth centuries. It wreaks havoc with all individualistic values: it is not a "live and let live" attitude. It does not say "it doesn't matter what you believe as long as you're sincere." It does not believe that Christian values are purely subjective, each person negotiating her or his own values with God in private. It calls for the renunciation of all deep attachments to what the world holds dear: goods, social advancement, the satisfaction of appetites at the expense of others, the right to dominate others in any personal relationship.

But if humility is hard, it is also powerful. Humility has to do with taking and accepting radical responsibility for the things that happen in life.

Abba John the Dwarf said, "Who sold Joseph into Egypt?" A brother replied, saying, "It was his brothers." "No!" the old man said to him. "It was his humility, because he could have said, 'I am their brother,' and have objected, but because he kept silent, he sold himself by his humility. It is also his humility which set him up as chief in Egypt." (Apoth., John the Dwarf 20, p. 90)

According to these fathers, Joseph's refraining from acting in his own selling into Egypt, and his insistence on giving up ordinary apparently self-serving ways in Egypt put him in a position to wield much power in Egypt and to provide for his family during the famine in Palestine. About John the Dwarf himself it was said, "Who is this John, who by his humility has all Scetis hanging from his little finger?" (Apoth., John the Dwarf 36, p. 93). These fathers and mothers were always in the thick of things. They ruled Egypt, like Joseph. Their influence in the ancient world was awe-inspiring. Crowds of people flocked to them for advice, not just on religious matters, but in all matters regarding human relationships and even property, and the crowds included emperors, bishops, and generals, as well as common people.

Part of the power of humility comes from its letting go of the need to look good in the eyes of ourselves or of others. But another part of its power stems from what is its realism: humility knows already that force is not effective against violence, and if it is not effective, then force is not realistic either. If the world is to be changed, the promise of the Prince of Peace is that it will be by the adoption of a whole new set of values that stand in opposition to those of the world.

> They said of Abba Macarius the Egyptian that one day he went up from Scetis to the mountain of Nitria. As he approached the place he told his disciple to go on ahead. . . . [There, the disciple] met a priest of the pagans. The brother shouted after him, saying, "Oh, oh, devil, where are you off to?" The priest turned back and beat him, and left him half dead. Then, picking up his stick, [the Pagan] fled. When [that Pagan] had gone a little further, Abba Macarius met him running and said to him, "Greetings, greetings, you weary man!" Quite astonished, the other came up to him and said, "What good do you see in me, that you greet me this way?" The old man said to him, "I have seen you wearing yourself out without knowing that you are wearing yourself out in vain." The other said to him, "I will not let you go till you have made me a monk." *Through him, many Pagans became Christians. So Abba Macarius said, "One evil word makes even the good evil, while one good word makes even the evil good."* (Italics mine. Apoth., Macarius the Great 39, p. 137)

Part of the realism of humility is its conviction that every one of us, being human, is prone to sin. We suffer congenitally from a weakness in the face of temptation, and a lack of purity of motives.

This means we must watch ourselves and our motives. We must not allow ourselves to feel that we have "risen above" temptation, nor allow ourselves to be shocked when we meet sin in ourselves or others. Humility does not abandon its commitments; it does not indulge itself in the luxury of disillusionment. In short, it is humility that goes hand in hand with love, that makes love finally possible in such a jagged world as ours.

Chapter 4

The Passions

Humility was one of the chief monastic attitudes of heart which enabled a person to love. Yet our ancestors were convinced that love does not simply spring from humility, or the cultivation of any other virtue, attitude, or activity. Love is neither a matter of learning what to do and then doing it, nor is it a gift God bestows on us all at once. We begin to learn what love is, and to cultivate in ourselves what fosters it, but we also have to fight in ourselves what stands in the way of love.

Love has space to grow within us only as each of us learns to recognize, root out, or discipline within ourselves the conglomerate of obsessive emotions, attitudes, desires, and ways of acting that the monastics called "the passions." It is these passions that blind us in our dealings with ourselves, each other, and the world, and so pervert perfectly good and useful impulses which take away our freedom to love.

REVISIONING PASSION

As we found to be true with the word "humility," we twentieth-century Americans do not use "passion" or "passions" in the same way our ancestors did. For us, the word "passion" is used to refer to any very strong emotion, positive or negative. "She has a passionate desire to serve the poor." "He was in a real passion when he killed the man." "She is a passionate lover." "He has a passion for chocolates."

Furthermore, we have been reared to be heirs of an eighteenth-century culture which glorified reason and discounted emotion.

We have seen in our own century the equation of reason and science and we have had the two of them offered to us together as the ultimate and only hope for humanity. "Emotionalism" has been linked with childishness and self-indulgence. It is a blessing of our own time that so many of us have come to realize the dreadful damage that has been done to us and by us as we have accepted such an attitude toward human emotion. Men and women both are working hard to overcome crippling ingrained habits of thought and feeling. Even when we succeed, however, we know that the damage done has not been simply to individuals. However we view things at the personal level, we find ourselves living in a monstrous world that science has created and may very well destroy. We feel betrayed and outraged.

Fed up with the idealization of science and rationality, many of us have worked hard to learn to value our human emotions, especially strong emotions. We have found out the hard way that the man or woman who lives "rationally" at the expense of the heart is a wounded being who wounds others. We fear what we have been taught by popular psychology to call the repression of our feelings, and we want to welcome any strong emotion as proof that we are truly alive and untrammeled by a civilization that would have us deny who we are. We want to be full of a passion for life itself.

Our ancient monastic forebears are using the word "passion" in a different way. They would not speak of a passion for life. As a word, "passion" carries a negative meaning most of the time because for them a passion has as its chief characteristics the perversion of vision and the destruction of love. A passion may very well be a strong emotion, but it need not be. A passion can also be a state of mind, or even a habitual action. Anger is usually a passion, but sometimes forgetfulness is called a passion. Gossip and talking too much are also regularly called passions in this literature. Depression, the very opposite of a passion as we usually use that term in our modern world, is one of the most painful passions.

Strong emotions which accompany love, lead to love, or even are an expression of love are not passions. Real love, as opposed to manipulative love that serves the lover alone, produces more love rather than destroying love, and so it cannot be a passion. A strong desire to serve the poor will not be described as a passion in our literature. Mercy, hospitality, remorse so strong that it is accompanied by torrents of tears—none of these is called a "passion" because of their relationship to love. On the other hand, overreligiosity, scrupulousness about one's own righteousness to the point of seeing the neighbor as secondary to that righteousness, indifference to the well-being of others, a judgmental attitude— all these are "passions."

A GLIMPSE AT AN ANCIENT PSYCHOLOGY

The early Christians we are studying did not think all this up by themselves, nor did they get it by a revelation of God. Basically, they were working with a popular psychology that went back to Plato. One of the most frequent metaphors they used to illustrate the human makeup was that of a charioteer driving a chariot pulled by two horses. The two horses are two basic impulses or life forces within us which make us interact with our world by drawing things into ourselves and pushing ourselves against other things. These are called the "appetitive and the spirited," or desire and anger. (Gr.Life II, 96.)

The appetitive and the spirited, desire and anger, are far more fundamental than surface emotions, "I want the dress," "I am angry at that boy." They are two sources of energy, one bringing in the outside world to the self, the other pushing against it. What we ordinarily think of as desire and anger, sexual attraction and repulsion, compassion and contempt are fueled by these basic impulses. Anger and desire, as basic drives, are themselves blind. Though our participation in the life of God depends on them, they are not ours as human beings alone. We share these two basic internal sources of energy with all the other animals who have physical bodies. Without them we could not live. When these drives function as they are meant to they are good; they are part of our nature, given to us by God in our creation. They are the horses for our chariot.

Driving the chariot is reason. It is reason that enables human beings to see the world and respond to it not simply on a level of physical needs and desires, but consciously and morally. For the Christian monastics, this meant to see and know God, to see as God sees, and to love God and other people. Acts of compassion and forgiveness, worship, insight into others all stem from reason which is fueled by desire and anger. The horses provide the energy and power; it is the charioteer who sets the direction of the travel and puts the energy of the chariot in motion.

If reason is somehow overthrown by the horses, however, chaos results; the energy of the horses becomes the source of power for various destructive passions, and the human personality is turned over to these passions which victimize it and destroy it as they repeatedly try unsuccessfully to satisfy themselves. But they can never permanently fill themselves up: Gregory of Nyssa uses the metaphor of the brickmold that the Israelites in Egypt used to make brick to illustrate the passions' insatiability. Just as the mold was continually filled with mud for the brick and just as continually emptied out to be refilled, so are our desires when not governed by reason. Our human experience proves this to be true: fulfilling the lust for a new car this year will not prevent the same lust next year. Hardly anyone who has ever said "if only I could have a ----, I would be happy" has found it to be so. A life that takes its meaning from eating, or sex, or owning things can never be fulfilled because the desires can never be permanently satisfied. These desires are alternately filled and recurring over and over. This phenomenon has been called "the cycle of desire." Only with reason in control are the two basic energies good for us rather than hurtful.

This is not our twentieth-century understanding of reason, of course. For us, reason and logic are equated. Human beings reason, but computers do it even better. This is because we have come to believe that the opposite and enemy of reason are human emotions. Reason has to do with what is universally true everywhere and forever. Emotion is individual and particular and messy and essentially self-centered. We believe that a mother's love for her child blinds her to the truth about that child. A family's love for a patch of woods behind their house prevents them from seeing the good that would come to the neighborhood by the building of a chemical factory on that spot. A computer is not confused by such particular and blinding human emotions.

But note: in our ancient sources, human emotion is not the opposite of reason. The passions are the opposite of reason. Love, as we have already said, is linked with reason, not opposed to it. Reason *serves* love. Love draws reason to the good, to God. We moderns assume that love blinds because we believe that somehow we see people as they really are only when we see them at their worst. We know that secretly Mary is slovenly, or John is a crook, or Susan is only interested in herself. When we find people's flaws after a long acquaintance with them, we believe we are finally seeing the truth about them. Our Christian ancestors thought exactly the opposite: we see people as they really are only when we see them through the tender and compassionate eyes of God. The Macarian Homilies, for example, say this metaphorically: "If you see a [person] with one eye, do not make any judgment in your heart but regard him as though he were whole. See the crippled as straight, the paralytic as healthy" (Mac., Homily 15, 8, p. 96). It is this kind of vision that is essential to being truly rational.

A judgmental attitude, one of the worst of the passions, is in direct conflict, therefore, with reason. What is opposite to reason are the passions which are destructive of the positive emotions that enable us to be in the world without seeing everything and everybody in it as potential fuel for our own fire. It is the passions which blind us, not love or compassion or generosity or any of their relations.

This understanding of the passions does not fit our model of human psychology, but it can be useful to us if we remember that our way of speaking of the conscious and the unconscious, or the id, the ego, and the superego, or even the rational and the irrational are just as much ways of speaking as the ancient language of the rational, the appetitive, and the spirited. The human personality is complex, and it can be very helpful to be reminded that psychological *models* are only that—they are not scientific laws.

It is especially helpful to us in the present to see that rationality has been understood in a Christian context to be closely linked with love. If it is not, it is hard to see how it could have any intrinsic value in and of itself. For the Christian, God does not act as creator with a neutral attitude toward creation, and we must expect the very structures of reality to reflect God's love in creation. This does not mean that we expect that everything in our world is good and pain and suffering only illusory or even that in any given situation everything will turn out all right in the end. But it means that God's love is present in the very structures of the natural world itself, if only we can see it. Irenaeus, an important second-century Christian writer, goes so far as to say that the existence of the four directions—north, south, east, and west—which make up the shape of the cross, points to God's suffering love in creation itself, a love already there and only made visible in a particularly obvious way at the physical crucifixion of Jesus. The fourth-century theologian Athanasius makes the same point when he says that seeing

God in Christ serves to point us back to creation to see God there, for the first time, as God really is. This means that we can no longer regard our physical world as the secular sphere, somehow separate or even dangerous to the religious sphere. Instead, we are able to see God's love for the world shown forth in the love and delight of mothers and babies, the sacrifices parents make for children and friends for each other, the terrible grief we feel at the death of a child we bore and cared for.

THE PASSIONS AND THE BODY

This ancient model of psychology which we have been examining assumes that each person is composed of a body, which is physical, and a mind. (Sometimes the mind is divided into the soul, the blind life force that animates the body, and the spirit, or the thinking, feeling, conscious part of the human being.) The mind is limited by the body in ways that are sometimes in our control and sometimes not, but mind and body are linked together inseparably. There are some people whose opinions have been preserved from this period who seem to suggest that though mind and body are joined, our body is somehow not really "us." Such a negative way of regarding human physical life is a minority opinion, however, and one shared by pagan philosophers of the period. The Neoplatonic philosopher Plotinus, for example, would not allow his portrait to be painted because he was ashamed of being "in the body." For the most part, Christians, on the other hand, could not believe that we are basically spirits pinned down temporarily in our physical bodies. The church early on rejected such a position as a denial of God's goodness in creation, affirming in its creed, "we believe in the resurrection of the body."

In our own time, a good many of us feel suspicious of any way of viewing a human being as divided into soul and body, however much those who hold such a view say they want to affirm the goodness of the body. Modern science has already demonstrated that our minds are not separable from our bodies in the way we have often been taught to believe Christians of previous centuries thought. Those of us who were raised in a branch of Christianity that seemed to regret that Christians even had to have bodies may be especially suspicious. We had to work hard to like our bodies, to come to know that we are whole people, body and soul. Popular psychology supports our suspicions and reinforces our fears about what is called "body-soul dualism."

That our ancestors were wrong in their science, however, does not mean that their observation of human life was or is false. They knew that our physical existence limits us, causes us pain, and finally eventuates in our death, and while they understood the physical limitations of our life as "natural," they would not rejoice in these limitations. These very ancient words are recited during the Syrian Orthodox funeral service as though they come from the mouth of the dead person, and they contain no trace of our more common modern assertion that death is a natural part of life and is therefore to be accepted if not actually rejoiced in:

> Lovers and children, who has taken me away from among you? Sons and daughters, who has carried me away from your company? Weep for me and multiply your lamentations over me, for this same day is sending me down to the grave. (*The Order for the Burial of the Dead,* Syrian Orthodox Church [1974], p. 92)

Life is good, but it also holds great pain for us that we would be better off acknowledging than redescribing.

Abba Poemen said, "Because of our need to eat and sleep, we do not see the simple things" (Apoth., Poemen 132, p. 186). The need for sleep and food and the inevitability of death all are passions, though clearly not ones we are responsible for. If we remember that a passion has as its outstanding characteristic its ability to prevent love, we can understand why these physical needs are lumped with anger, envy, and boredom. A mother who has gotten up with a sick child a dozen times in the night, in her exhausted sleep may not hear the child when it cries one more time. A person hungry and tired, ready to leave work, may not be able to listen sympathetically to a co-worker's problem, if the person chooses to unburden at five o'clock. A forty-year-old cannot play basketball as he might like with a nineteen-year-old. Everyone has had the experience of feeling one age and looking in the mirror only to find an older person we see almost as a stranger. Our bodies have a life and timetable of their own over which we can exercise only limited control.

The early monastics' irritation at this state of affairs is the reason for a lot of what looks to us to be a hatred of the body. It was not that they hated their bodies; they simply did not wish to have their lives determined by their physical needs any more than they could help. Why sleep or eat more than you need? They believed we must train ourselves to be less dependent. We must take care of our necessities and not pamper our desire for self-indulgence or we will trap ourselves into being unhappy or even helpless once we are addicted to our pleasures. They thought we need to cut out variety in food to the point where we do not notice what we eat. Cut back on sleep so that we only get what we need. This seemingly dreary but practical advice often appeared in a blatantly impractical form: "Abba Arsenius used to say that one hour's sleep is enough for a monk if he is a good fighter" (Apoth., Arsenius 15, p. 11).

But the idea was to find the limits of our bodies, not punish them or eradicate them. Note this story of a monk who tried to go without sleep altogether:

> [Macarius of Alexandria] decided to be above the need for sleep, and he claimed that he did not go under a roof for twenty days in order to conquer sleep. He was burned by the heat of the sun and was drawn up with the cold at night. And he also said, "If I had not gone into the house and obtained the advantage of some sleep, my brain would have shrivelled up for good. I conquered to the extent that I was able, but I gave in to the extent my nature required sleep." (Pal. sec. 18, "Macarius of Alexandria," para. 3, p. 59)

Human beings are, in fact, limited by their physical bodies, in spite of what they might want, and ignoring those limitations will only lead to disaster.

Very few of the passions that we would expect the early monks to worry about were strictly passions of the body or passions of the mind, however. Because of the intimate nature of the relationship between body and mind, it was hard to lay the blame in one place rather than in both. Avarice, for example, according to Evagrius Ponticus, had its roots in a fear of death and sickness in old age, but also in an emotional inability to be dependent upon other people, even in imagining the future. Gluttony's roots were in a desire for variety in food—this is what got Adam and Eve in trouble—and such a desire is neither all physical nor all mental. Most of our passions, in fact, arise out of an intertwining of our knowledge of our physical limitations and our anxiety over them.

In general, the monastic was taught to dominate the body, that is, not to give in to all physical urges if those urges violated that person's desires and goals. On the other hand, they were taught to take care of the body; it is the only one they had and they could not do without it. Though early monastic notions of treating the body moderately would seem like self-torture for most of us, the *idea* they were espousing of limiting the body's unnecessary demands on us and their reasons for limiting those demands are still profoundly useful. How much of our lives have been spent uncomfortable and out of sorts because we did not have what we thought we needed when what we needed was not necessary either for our life or health—coffee, cigarettes, well-cooked food, or a trip being among the more obvious?

Furthermore, we have given ourselves a very serious problem our ancient ancestors did not have. In our own time, in which we jog and diet and generally believe that there must be an intimate connection between virtue, physical beauty, health, and a person's worth, we make outcasts of those among us who do not measure up: the old, the fat, the young but unattractive, the handicapped. That we have discovered that there is no real physical basis for believing in a "body-soul dualism" provides us with a reason to value people in terms of what they look like and what they are able to do physically. Our churches are as guilty of this amazing confusion as any other group. This is a theology of "wholeness" that benefits the strong and ignores the weak. It certainly stands in opposition to the Christian way of life we are exploring together in these pages.

THE PASSIONS AND THE LOSS OF FREEDOM

The passions blind us so that we cannot love. They create for us interior lenses through which we see the world, lenses which we very often do not even know are there. When we are under the control of our passions, even when we think we are most objective, we cannot be—we are in the grip of emotions, states of mind, habits that distort everything we see. What we think of as love while we are in the grip of the passions may very well have little to do with the person we supposedly love.

Envy is a particularly difficult passion. For example, suppose I have a neighbor who is younger than I; this hypothetical neighbor has a job that pays three times what mine pays; she has lovely clothes and a big house, and prospers in everything she does. I, on the other hand, am middle-aged. What has come to me with great difficulty has come to her easily, so easily that she rather looks down on my own battle scars from life. One day, gossip begins to float around the neighborhood that her marriage is in trouble. I listen with interest, telling myself that I wish her no harm and I will not pass on the gossip. Nevertheless, I feel a sense of satisfaction, ever so slight. She deserves to get in trouble. Envy makes me see her through a haze made up of my own desire for power, my resentment that my life has not been as easy as hers seems, my sense of inadequacy next to her apparent perfections, a touch of humiliation, and a straightforward desire for what she has that a secret part of me wishes that I had. I may wish to love her, may tell myself that I do love her, but I do *not* see her objectively, whatever I might tell myself, and this distortion inhibits my loving her.

Depression, which is a passion in this literature, distorts our vision with even more disastrous results, as most people know who have ever suffered from it. Depression steals the joy from our work and our play. Depression can make all of life seem flat and empty, everything and everybody boring, the mattress lumpy, and food without taste. Good people can appear to us to be hypocrites and cynical people who place no value on human life can seem to be the only realists. In such a frame of mind we see our own lives as worthless, no good to ourselves or to anyone else. The worse the depression, the more separated we feel from others, and the harder it is to see ourselves as well as other people as we all really are.

If the way we see ourselves and other people is distorted by our passions, our way of seeing God is just as distorted. A person who feels resentful and angry a lot of the time at herself and other people is not likely to experience God as loving and forgiving. A person who hates women is not likely to experience God in feminine terms as well as masculine. Where the dominant image of God is as lawgiver and judge, God's mercy will surely seem inaccessible. This is why the early monastics insist that we do not really love God from the day we first become Christian: we may love the little glimpse that we see, but we cannot love God as God really is because our vision is too distorted. We can only grow into love as the power of the passions weakens.

Most of us consider the ability to feel and express passions a kind of freedom. It feels liberating to throw a cup down on the kitchen floor and break it in a rage, and in one sense it is, if you have been angry a long time and not acknowledged it. But the literature suggests that the passions blind us, and thus take away our freedom. The anger that explodes all at once is already there and doing its destructive work before the explosion. Such an expression of rage, especially when it bursts out of us unexpectedly, is hardly freedom, and it certainly does not end the anger. In fact, there is psychological evidence now that the "free" expression of anger feeds the anger, rather than putting it to an end.

If we see ourselves or other people one way, and they are actually very different from what we see, we cannot make real choices about what we see. A person convinced the whole world is out to get him is not free to believe that many people wish him well or are not interested in him at all. A smoker addicted to cigarettes will tell you sincerely that there is no proof that smoking causes lung cancer, and besides, we all have to die of something, anyway. A kind of self-induced blindness has taken away her freedom. The pressure family and friends exert on a young couple to marry often results in a disastrous marriage because wanting to please others and be seen as a good and successful person often itself becomes a blinding passion, as one or both of the partners in the potential marriage discount the signs to themselves that the marriage is almost sure to be unhappy.

Real freedom comes from being able to see what the actual choices are in any given situation, and then to be able to choose and act on the choices. Freedom means freedom to love. It has little to do with what we think of as freedom as children, freedom to be as bad as we want. That comes rather easily for most of us if we are given the chance. Loving is another matter.

THE PASSIONS, TEMPTATION, SIN AND THE DEMONS

Where do the passions come from? Are they a natural part of us? Are they the same as temptation? What do they have to do with sin?

When we turn to the literature of the early church for the first time, it is bound to seem to us to be full of demons and/or the devil. Jesus is tempted by the devil in the wilderness in the gospels. He casts out demons into a herd of swine. He heals people possessed of demons. Demons appear to us everywhere. The fourth-century literature of early monasticism carries on the belief of the culture in demons and associates them with the passions and temptation.

Actually, the early literature itself demonstrates a great variety of thought about the demons and their connection with the passions. The early part of the *Life of St. Anthony* is overrun with them, as they appear to him in various disguises such as a beautiful and seductive girl, and a small black boy. At their worst, he meets them in a tomb where he goes to wrestle deliberately with them as they personify the forces of death and destruction. They are not merely symbolic, either, as they knock him out with great shouting and other noise. Finally he defeats them by persistently standing up to them and refusing to submit to them. For Anthony the demons have a real existence as hostile beings exterior to himself. He explains (or rather, his biographer explains), however, that they really have no supernatural power. They cannot get into our minds to read our thoughts; instead, they watch us carefully, and read our body language! They are not able to predict the future, he says, as some people who consult pagan oracles think. They operate by running very fast to other places and then running back to report what they have found, and all of this is by natural means. Not all ancient sources would seem to agree with these details about the activity, but they would agree about this most important fact of demon lore: the demons have no more power over us than we grant to them. They are unspeakably malicious and diabolically clever but they are only able to attack us at points of vulnerability. They have no power at all to make us feel or do what we do not assent to. They do, however, have the power to tempt us.

Seemingly at the opposite end of the spectrum we find a statement like the following:

> Abraham, the disciple of Abba Agathon, questioned Abba Poemen saying, "How do the demons fight against me?" Abba Poemen said to him, "The demons fight against you? They do not fight against us at all as long as we are doing our own will. For our own wills become the demons, and it is these which attack us in order that we may fulfill them. But if you want to see who the demons really fight against, it is against Moses and those who are like him." (Apoth., Poemen 67, p. 176)

According to Abba Poemen, ordinary people and monks have no experience of demons at all. Rather, their temptations come not from any external demons but from themselves, from their own choices, their own wills. Only the great holy women and holy men of history had to deal with demons. Presumably the rest of us cave in to our desires too quickly for the demons to want to bother with us. Evagrius Ponticus, the fourth-century writer whose analysis of the passions contributed a good deal to the medieval discussion of the seven deadly sins, displays little interest in the demons. As far as he is concerned, it is the psychological elements of the passions a monk should attend to, not the demonic. His writings will prove particularly helpful to us in the next chapter.

Of far more importance for the modern reader than the question of demons, no matter how interesting, is that of temptation and its connection with the passions. In our own perspective, we often confuse temptation to "sin" with the act itself. The fantasy of going after the boss with a bullwhip may leave us feeling as guilty as we imagine we would feel if we actually took the whip to him or her. Even though we do not express it, that an angry retort should come into our head under provocation strikes us as a breach of Christian love. After all, Jesus himself said that if we commit adultery in our heart we as good as do it, and if we call our brother a numbskull we can expect to be judged for it.

Again, the Christians of the early church were more subtle than we are. Though there were a few people who thought the "perfect" Christian no longer had trouble with temptations and the passions, not many believed it. We can expect temptations as long as we live. Some thought these temptations were the same ones we have to struggle with all through life: if a temptation to lose your temper or to laziness plagues you when you are fifteen, it will plague you, perhaps in a different form, when you are fifty. Others thought that we go from temptation to temptation as we begin to bring the passions under control one at a time.

But a temptation is neither a passion nor a sin. What we really have no control over we are not responsible for. The images that arise in our minds, our spontaneous moods, these we are never free of. It is only when we seize hold of the thought or the image or the mood, brooding on it and feeding it and encouraging it to grow, that we become responsible. This is the point where it starts to become a passion. Though a full-blown passion seems to have a life of its own while we are held helpless in its grip, the contention is that passions do not start with this kind of power over us. A vague dislike for another person can easily be fanned by us into an active resentment that sets the mood for a whole day. A nudge of envy can be turned into a vicious desire to gossip. A sexual attraction toward another person can grow into an obsession if fantasies are given free rein.

Passions have a developmental process of their own. Someone

once asked Abba Poemen about what "do not repay evil for evil"
(1 Thess. 5:15) means and in reply he outlined the process of
growth a passion goes through from its beginnings to its full-grown
stage:

> . . . "Passions work in four stages—first, in the heart; secondly, in
> the face; thirdly, in words; and fourthly, it is essential not to render
> evil for evil in deeds. If you can purify your heart, passion will not
> come into your expression; but if it comes into your face, take care
> not to speak; but if you do speak, cut the conversation short in case
> you render evil for evil." (Apoth., Poemen 34, p. 172)

At each stage we have the choice of allowing the passion to grow
into the next stage or of preventing it. Temptation comes to us
whether we choose it or not, but in the case of the passions, they
do not overwhelm us all at once in the same way.

As for sin, this literature speaks very little about it. Temptations
are not sins. Passions are destructive of our ability to love, and
they are quite likely to cause harm to the neighbor who is to be
the object of that love, and for that we are responsible. But sin
itself, called by that name, appears infrequently in these writings.
There is little sense that God is hurt or offended by our human
passions; it is we who are God's image who are injured. Conse-
quently, though references to judgment day occur frequently, to
most of the monastics God's mercy is far more evident than God's
justice.

NAMING THE PASSIONS

We have just seen something of the passions and how they blind
us so that we are not able to see people, God, or things as they
really are. Now it is time to see what the individual passions are
that our ancestors were concerned about and how they took their
toll on them and still take their toll on us. The passions as the
monastics describe them do not belong only to a few human beings
with serious problems. Though we all suffer from the passions in
different combinations and in different strengths, we do, indeed,
all suffer from the passions. The lives of all of us are distorted by
the passions.

We come up against several temptations when we are faced with
our own passions. We want to look around to find others worse
off or better than we, to see that we are not so bad compared with
some, or to decide that we are so bad off that our case is hopeless.

But this is to miss the point. We talk about the passions in the first place in order to begin to get free of them, not to make anyone feel helplessly inadequate or guilty. Certainly our discussion ought not to give anyone a weapon for naming and lording it over other people's weaknesses. We name the passions as an important step toward our own freedom to love.

Everyone talked about the passions in the early period of the church. It was not a particularly religious way of talking about difficulties of human life; it was simply part of the psychology of the day, as we saw in the previous chapter. Men and women in the desert fought the passions since the time of Saint Anthony. Before that, they fought them at home. The first systematic list of the passions, however, with some discussion on where they came from and how to fight them came from a particularly interesting fourth-century monk named Evagrius Ponticus. It is Evagrius's list that forms the basis of the medieval list of the seven deadly sins and it is the one we will work from. Needless to say, it is not exhaustive. Other passions appear in the literature, and any of us may have problems at any given time with passions that we do not discuss here.

Gluttony

Gluttony is the first passion Evagrius lists. Evagrius and many others in the ancient world were convinced the first sin of Adam and Eve was gluttony. Gluttony was a broad term for the monastics. It meant, of course, overeating, but more fundamentally, it was connected with a desire for a lot of unnecessary variety in food. Gluttony suggested an obsession with food that had nothing to do with actual physical need. It is also connected by Evagrius with hypochondria, a fear that if one does not eat what one wants, one will become ill. Gluttony is about letting food control us, occupying time and attention that needs to be given more profitably elsewhere.

For us, Evagrius's notion of gluttony can be very useful. If gluttony has to do with an obsession with food, we certainly suffer from it as a culture. Nutritionists tell us we need variety in what we eat, which the ancients did not know. Nevertheless, especially for those of us responsible for the care and feeding of families, an enormous amount of our time and/or money is spent planning meals, shopping, cooking, eating, and cleaning up. Many of us are so obsessed with our health that a great deal of energy and money goes into health food or excessive exercise that will not really benefit us much. When we think of gluttony as an obsession with food that blinds us and prevents love, anorexia nervosa appears as an especially dangerous variety of gluttony, since its sufferers apparently lose even an accurate vision of what their bodies look like. I believe we could profitably wonder if gluttony is not as central to most of us as it seemed to be to our ancient ancestors, especially in the light of the starvation that is prevalent all over the world. Why do we not share our resources?

Avarice

As Evagrius defines it, avarice means being unwilling to share your resources with others. It stems, first, from a fear of the future: if I give away what I have now, what will happen to me when I am old? What if I become ill and have nothing to provide for myself? Second, it stems from an unwillingness to accept help from others if we should come to be in need later.

Remember, the passions create blindness. If we look at Evagrius's concept of avarice in modern terms, we see that Evagrius would not tell people like ourselves not to worry about planning for the future. He is speaking, however, to all those who save for a rainy day that never comes. He also speaks to those who can never give to others without a painful but unrealistic sense of being deprived themselves, or having put themselves in danger. Avarice has to do with believing that possessions actually provide far more security than they do, a very common misconception in our materialistic culture.

The other element of avarice for the monastic was shame at receiving charity. Not only does our culture make a virtue of never being in need; it tends to be contemptuous of those who *are* in need, materially or emotionally. But it is those who recognize that they are in need who are able to approach Jesus in the gospels. An independence that is too proud to ask for or receive help is never praised. To overcome this particular passion is truly to see the world with different eyes.

Impurity

This is the hardest passion to discuss because it did not exactly mean to the ancient monastics what it means to us. Evagrius calls it "lusting after bodies," and in its simplest state it drove the ancient monastic, who was vowed to celibacy, to engage in sexual acts. At its more fundamental level, however, it pushed one into the temptation to leave the monastic life for marriage. But the monastics regarded the celibate life as a fundamental act of faith in the face of death: because they believed in the fulfilling of God's promises, they would have no need of a partner to console them because of their mortality. Nor would they need children to carry on their lives after they themselves died. Giving in to lust was an abandonment of hope for the sake of physical gratification.

Few of us consciously look at sex and marriage in this light. Nevertheless, our sexuality continues to distort our modern vision. People marry who ought not to marry merely because of sexual attraction. Teenagers have babies out of wedlock. Families and even good marriages are broken up because of the sexual obsession of one of the married partners with another person with whom they may not even have anything in common.

Depression, Sadness

Few of us would think of depression as a passion, but to those who suffer from it, it should be immediately apparent that it is one of the most debilitating passions of all. When we are depressed we cannot see ourselves as beloved children of God, regardless of what we do or do not do. Our way of seeing ourselves, our past lives, and our accomplishments, not to mention our way of seeing all around us, is distorted and colored gray by our depression. Usually we even know our vision is distorted, but we cannot find the energy to fight against it.

Evagrius roots depression in a kind of grief for what has been given up for the sake of the present life. For the monastic, it may stem from a knowledge that he or she will never have a family, or a memory of past comforts or past honors. For us it might manifest itself as regret that we did not marry another person, or remain single, or have children, or go without children, or choose a different profession. The content of the nostalgic regret is not important, so much as the ability of this depression to leach out everything positive from our perception of life. Whether we agree with Evagrius's analysis of where depression comes from, there is no question that it is one of the most destructive and painful of all the passions.

Anger

Evagrius calls anger "the most fierce passion," and there is probably more in the monastic literature about the destructive nature of anger than all the rest of the passions put together. That is because, in the opinion of our ancestors, anger is more potentially destructive of love than any other passion. Furthermore, there is more danger of self-deception, as we tell ourselves we are correcting others for their own good. But as Poemen says, "Instructing one's neighbor is for the [person] who is whole and without passions; for what is the use of building the house of another, while destroying one's own?" (Apoth., Poemen 127, p. 185). Resentments, short and long, interfere with prayer and prevent us from even approaching God as they absorb our energy and attention.

In our own modern culture, we are given support for believing that anger is somehow good for us, and its expression even better. But many studies indicate that expressing anger does not make it go away. Further, even if expressing anger did remove it, if the relationship with the object of our anger has been broken or damaged by our expression, we have defeated our Christian goal of love. Evagrius recommends, instead, the persistent attempt at a resolution of whatever problem it was that created the anger in the first place. But this attempt at resolution cannot be based in a feeling of superiority over the offender. It is true that not all situations can be resolved in such a way that love is not broken; nevertheless, most of us give up much too easily.

Evagrius also discusses occasions when we are angered by another, but a little voice says to us, Christians do not argue; if I do not mention it, it will be all right tomorrow. According to Evagrius, this is not a virtue, it is a temptation. Anger does not go away on its own; if a problem arises with a person with whom we are intimate, we *must* talk with the person toward whom we feel that anger. A good many marriages and friendships and even churches would be greatly improved if we took Evagrius seriously at this point.

Acedia

The name of this passion comes to us via the Middle Ages as sloth, but sloth suggests laziness, which this is not. Acedia is a restless boredom that makes our ordinary tasks seem too dull to bear. Evagrius says it makes "the day [seem] fifty hours long." Nothing seems right; life has lost its savor and it all seems somebody else's fault, so that the only alternative is to leave everything and go off somewhere else. According to a famous statement of Abba Moses only persistently sticking it out in the same place will cure this acedia: "sit in your cell and your cell will teach you everything" (Apoth., Moses 6, p. 139).

Acedia is as debilitating now as it was then. We experience it as a restlessness that sometimes makes us hate our jobs. Some experience it as boredom with a marriage that they seek to cure with affairs. Others change residences at periodic intervals or take up dangerous hobbies or go out and spend money. Whatever the attempted solution tried, however, the feeling is the same: an empty, restless boredom with life itself.

This restlessness often stems from one of two sources. First, acedia often comes from one degree or another of exhaustion from too little sleep or not enough leisure. Nothing can sap an interest in life like chronic tiredness. In this case, Evagrius's advice may be helpful in some ways, unhelpful in others. A mother and father of a toddler may not be able to leave town until the baby is older; they have to tough it out. On the other hand, they may not have taken their need for breaks from the baby seriously enough to do something about it. If the need for leisure is the source of the problem, many people aggravate their acedia by filling their spare time with more and more activities that do not give rest. Here Evagrius's advice can be useful if we interpret it to mean "find a time and place to be quiet. Allow breathing time every day. Do not let prayer be replaced by frantic activity."

Acedia often has a second cause. We often try to find meaning in life from things that do not give ultimate meaning: work, marriage, friendships, hobbies, material possessions. Poemen's advice is, "Do not give your heart to that which does not satisfy the heart" (Apoth., Poemen 80, p. 178). All of these things are good and important, but they are not ultimate. Of course we cannot find our deepest self in them. We are not made that way. Only God, finally, can satisfy our bored and restless hearts so that we are able to love.

Vainglory

Liking praise or recognition, or needing to be liked so much that our actions are determined by our need, is the passion of vainglory. In ancient monasticism, its sufferers needed to be conspicuous in their ascetical practices or their prayers, or whatever else it was that made people admire them. Suffering from vainglory, that admiration, instead of love of God and their fellow human beings, became the goal of their lives.

Vainglory is a particularly insidious passion in our modern era.

It lies behind the notion that whatever your skills, it is essentially yourself you are selling to others. Women are trained to please as little girls, and many women suffer from it all their lives to such an extent that they are not aware of any needs of their own, except to be approved of or loved. It is a special passion for ministers and priests and teachers, and anyone else whose self-identity is bound up in the idea of service. It is deceptively easy to confuse being liked with having done a good job. Vainglory is probably at the root of a lot of burn-out as the desire for approval replaces the goals of the vocation; certainly an enormous amount of self-deception, and hence blindness, stem from vainglory.

Pride

Pride is the last of Evagrius's passions. It is the inverse of humility. It manifests itself as a devaluing of others as we compare ourselves to those around us. In modern terms, it makes up an important part of envy. Its essential quality is not found in having too high an opinion of oneself so much as too low an opinion of everyone else. Self-righteousness is one of its more obnoxious characteristics, as its sufferer looks around to make sure the people around her or him are as good as they ought to be. It begins in a little satisfaction as someone around us pays for what he or she may have done wrong. It ends with its sufferer finding value in nothing in the universe, not even God, except that which directly benefits her or him.

On the passion of pride the ancients are more modern than we might wish. Human pride taints everything it touches. It is the absolute and implacable enemy of love, and only humility is its antidote. If only Evagrius were not so excruciatingly relevant!

CONCLUSION

Most of us are not done in by our great passions, by our towering rages, by hiding shoeboxes of money under the bed, or by our sneering contempt for the rest of the human race. The assumption in the early literature is that it is the little things we do over a long period of time that form character and make our relationships with ourselves, others, and God what they are. This is why some of what we read could appear to be nit-picking. Why does an Abba worry about his disciple picking up a dried pea that does not belong to him off the road? Not because a good monk is so scrupulous, but because the great and seemingly uncontrollable passions do not start out ready-made. They begin with small things that we tell ourselves do not matter: a general snappishness toward family members when we have had a hard day, a sense of self-satisfaction when someone we do not care for gets what is coming to them. This is where we all make mistakes. We are offended that someone should take a small act of inconsiderateness on our part as a sign of our lack of care for them, when, in fact, they are right. This is where our passions begin.

We turn to a more cheerful subject, the role of introspection and prayer in the defeat of the passions.

Chapter 5

Prayer

If the passions are the enemies of our ability to love other people and God, how do we fight them? Our early monastic forebears had many ways to do this, but two of the most helpful to us are prayerful introspection and prayer itself.

INTROSPECTION

Introspection means looking inside ourselves to see what it is that makes us tick or fails to make us tick in order that we may love. It has to do with observing ourselves to see what we think or feel or do that hurts us or makes us hurt others *so that we can do something about what needs to be corrected, and strengthen what needs to be strengthened.* It involves acknowledging how complex we all are as we try to move in several often conflicting directions at once. Wallowing in guilt or helplessness for its own sake is not what introspection is about, according to our literature.

The monastics assumed that all of us know ourselves at some level much better than we want to admit we do. No matter how blinded by passions we are to ourselves, other people, and God, there always is a little bit of us that can see the truth. Nevertheless, we often do not care to see it, and so we use up a lot of energy hiding from that seeing part of ourselves and denying what it sees. We know the damage we are doing to ourselves and other people with our anger or hatred or our gluttony.

That part of us which is not destroyed or bent out of shape by the passions, that can still perceive the truth about ourselves and our world, early monastics speak of as the partially covered over but still existing image of God. To them one of the most important components of this human image of God in each one of us is our ability to look inside ourselves, acknowledging what we know and identifying with this part of ourselves that is the image of God.

Significantly, they speak of this characteristic of the image of God as sharing God's freedom to make choices. Obviously, in order to be able to have real freedom, people need to know what their real options are. But how can we ever make any real choices if we are so completely in the grip of and blinded by our passions that we cannot even see glimmers of those options?

This certainly does *not* mean that the monastics thought that, since we can almost always see the truth, no matter how faintly, we should just grit our teeth and overcome our passions by self-control. They knew that we are all like Paul: even when self-deception does not get in our way, much of the time the good that we want to do we cannot, and the evil we do not want to do, we cannot seem to help doing (Rom. 7:19). Often self-deception keeps right on functioning even when a part of us knows better. We know that our clothes are tight from overeating, or our children are irritable because we have been snapping at them, but we still tell ourselves the clothes shrank in the wash, and our kids are *always* in a bad mood in the morning, and so we cannot seem to change our behavior.

Being able to look inside ourselves and see what is going on is a crucial part of breaking free of the passions. The first monastics repeated in many forms the old Greek saying "know yourself" and they meant it. Poemen said, "Not understanding what has happened prevents us from going on to something better" (Apoth., Poemen 200, p. 194). Watch yourself as you interact with others and the world around you and puzzle over what you see until you know what your passions are: pride or depression or restless boredom, or whatever else. If you have trouble making sense of your passions, keep a record of the circumstances which give you the most trouble. Evagrius Ponticus suggests as part of this process that you notice whether certain passions appear at the same time of day every day. Then, he says, "ask Christ for an explanation" (E.P. Prak. 50, p. 30). By this he means be very attentive to the details of your life that accompany your passions: perhaps irritability is connected with too little sleep, perhaps it occurs when you get too much salt in your diet, or right before dinner. Intense anxiety may be seasonal, connected with the start of school or Christmas pressures; depression may hit predictably at the end of winter when you become convinced that spring will never come again. Or depression can hit when you are around people who make you feel helpless. It could be that your restless boredom comes when you are procrastinating about doing something you need to do. Looking inside and seeing these things is the first step away from the passions.

Use your time of introspection to find your own real needs. Too many times as Christians we believe we have a problem with, say, irritability, and we try to conquer the irritability head on, by prayer and self-control. But the truth may be that we are not taking seriously our own anger at something that needs to be corrected. The passion of anger is not hiding reality from us, but rather it is our fear of anger and lack of humility in the form of low self-esteem that needs to be tackled. Real needs that are not met are among the sources of the passions—a need for rest and quiet, for prayer, for leisure, for food and sleep.

Besides keeping a journal, there is another way of dealing with the passions that comes out of introspection. In the last chapter we saw the early psychological understanding of the irascible element, anger in its most fundamental form, as basic to all life. Evagrius explains that as human beings we have been given the irascible element as a major weapon against the passions. Before prayer, he says, stand back from yourself, imaginatively speaking, and rebuke your passion. Learn to say "you are my jealousy speaking," for example. "My feelings of fear and hurt may come from my past, but I will not let you control me."

Often, however, we are not able to see what is causing our problem, or if we can, the information is not helpful. We may not even know we have a problem. The ancient monastics helped themselves around their blindness with the help of their Amma or Abba. For them, having a teacher and guide was of real importance to the process of learning to escape from their own distortions of reality in order to learn to love. Here, for instance, is an exchange between a disciple and an Abba.

> A brother went to see Abba Poemen and said to him, "What ought I to do?" The old man said to him, "Go and join one who says 'What do I want?' and you will have peace." (Apoth., Poemen 143, p. 187)

The brother who came for help was caught in a way of looking at things that was oriented toward action; he believed that whatever his problems, he would solve them by *doing* something. His Abba, however, could see that, while the brother might be good at action, he was caught in a trap. Until he could choose a goal for himself by learning how to ask "what do I want?" he would not make any progress.

A person chose an Abba or an Amma and worked with him or her precisely because that teacher could be expected to have an intimate knowledge both of the disciple and of the struggle that comes with trying realistically to make progress in love. This knowledge helped the teacher to understand the disciple and help the disciple to avoid self-deception. This could be a terribly painful process:

> At first, Abba Ammoes said to Abba Isaiah [his disciple], "What do you think of me now?" He said to him, "You are an angel, Father." Later on he said to him, "And now what do you think of me?" He replied, "You are like Satan. Even when you say a good word to me, it is like steel." (Apoth., Ammoes 2, p. 30)

It was not that Ammoes changed his personality as his disciple worked with him. The disciple had found that being confronted by the Abba and rooting out self-deception could be excruciating.

Very few of us have an Amma or Abba today, but we are still in need of people we trust outside ourselves who, when we are in trouble, or trying to grow in the Christian life, or both, can tell us what they see us thinking or feeling or doing. Theoretically, if we had no alternative, it would be possible to be a Christian in isolation from other Christians, but it would also be a very sad thing. Christians need each other. Fortunately, even without an Amma or Abba the place of the teacher for us can in many ways be taken by our Christian community.

Ideally, this often happens in worship. Sometimes the words of scripture or prayer or even the sermon or homily can cut right through our self-deception to speak the truth to us: we might be jolted out of a fearful and helpless frame of mind, for example, by hearing the words of Psalm 46:

> God is our refuge and strength,
> a very present help in trouble.
> Therefore we will not fear though the earth should change,
> though the mountains shake in the heart of the sea . . .

Just as important, we also need to be able to count on individual friends, or a group of friends within our Christian community to function in this way for us. If we cannot, we must seek out friends like this to help us see inside ourselves without angrily judging us or suggesting to us their superiority to us. We need them to treat us gently and to be truthful with us. If they are Christian friends, they will share our goals, but if they are not, we still need them to share a portion of our vision of what we want for ourselves.

Of course, our friends cannot really be Ammas and Abbas as the ancient desert folk knew them; Ammas and Abbas were expected to be much farther along in the Christian life than their disciples, while our friends are likely to be fairly close to where we are. Furthermore, the ancient teachers asked for obedience from the disciples who were being trained in a rigorous way of life the teacher knew far more about than the student. But if we care about each other, we also have some knowledge of each other that we should be glad to share if asked, and if we are truly blessed, we have friends who will tell us what they see sometimes, even if we do not ask.

The ancient disciple *did* ask, however: she or he would approach the teacher and say "give me a word," and the teacher would respond according to the individual need of the moment. We, too, need to be able to seek out friends of this sort. Most of us are sensitive to criticism, and many of us have experienced the failure of friendships or intimate relations in which we have felt badly misunderstood or even betrayed. Unfortunately, friends usually do not happen along without our taking at least enough hand in the friendship to take some risks.

Somehow, in most of our churches, we are not prepared to take enough risks with each other. We are afraid of offending, afraid of sounding judgmental, and we are afraid of judgmentalism with good reason (the Abbas and Ammas were convinced that nothing drives another person away from God and other people faster than being on the receiving end of *any* kind of self-righteous criticism). Fear of judgmentalism is not the problem most of the time, however; church groups many times radiate such an air of "real Christians don't have problems" or "if you love the Lord, you rejoice always" that there is very little room for truthfulness among people who need to be able to be truthful with each other in order to grow into real love. The ancient monastics were convinced that having to struggle with the passions is part of everyone's human condition, so that we all can expect to have problems of one sort or another. We will experience them or at least be seriously tempted by them as long as we live, and we need our friends to help us by being real with us.

In our search for friends with whom to grow in the Christian life, we must be prepared to state our need, openly, to people who may be embarrassed by it. In the various "mainline" Protestant traditions, people rarely speak together of their prayer or their struggles as Christians, and there is no way to expect to find such helpful friends unless we overcome that reluctance which is almost a taboo. Considering the strength of that taboo, there is a surprising number of people who do feel a starvation for this kind of companionship. It will almost certainly feel awkward at first, and it may continue to be a bit uncomfortable until you are both used to it. It is well worth the discomfort, fear of embarrassment, and the work because being a Christian can never be a matter of only ourselves and God. We are part of the body of Christ, and need the other parts as well.

Being able to look into ourselves deeply takes real humility, and this does not mean acknowledging merely that we are sinners. It is true that we are sinners, but it is equally true that each of us is vulnerable in all sorts of ways, and God who made each one of us also loves each one of us in all our fragility. This means that we need not feel set apart from others by whatever introspection or conversation turns up within us, no matter what it is.

Cultivating humility also means that we will begin to stop measuring ourselves continually against others—a problem ancient Christians had, too, judging by the many times it is mentioned in the literature:

> Abba Poemen said that a brother who lived with some other brothers asked Abba Bessarion, "What ought I to do?" The old man said to him, "Keep silence and do not always be comparing yourself to others." (Apoth., Poemen 79, p. 178)

Having humility will mean that we will have no particular desire to do better than others, and we will not care if someone else does better than we. Pride hurts, but humility takes the fear out of a lot of introspection, making us courageous and strong.

Having the old virtue of humility also makes us patient with ourselves when we do find the things we probably will see in ourselves. We will be able to accept it as true that the passions, feelings, attitudes, obsessions, and certain kinds of behavior do not go away all at once simply because we have identified them.

Humility reminds us that the process of becoming free of our passions is often a long one, and that is all right. Humility allows us to follow another common piece of advice in the early monastic literature: do not try to do everything at once; take on only one passion at a time. Learning to love is a slow business.

Humility, finally, will enable us to hear what others tell us and will help us cultivate within ourselves a continuous attitude of listening to the world around us, to friends, to those who are not so friendly, to what we encounter in prayer and worship. Humility makes us receptive of all that comes to us that might bring us to love of God and of each other. Humility is the only possible attitude out of which we can ever speak a word of truth to another person without doing terrible harm to ourselves and the other. After all, what we are about is never ever executing God's righteous judgment on another person or ourselves.

PRAYER

Introspection and prayer are so integrally connected for the Christian that they are never completely separable. This is because as we are consciously introspective, Christian introspection is done, not for its own sake, as though we are infinitely interesting in ourselves to ourselves. Christian introspection is meant to lead to love, the love of God and the love of other people. This kind of healing introspection is always done in the presence of God, even if we are not always consciously aware of it. It is the presence of God when we look inside ourselves that makes real introspection possible. On the one hand, it is our knowledge of God's mercy and love for us which gives us the courage to attempt it in the first place. On the other hand, it is our deep sense of God's unending acceptance and concern for us that enables us to know that, whatever we find in ourselves, we will be able to bear the knowledge and ask in prayer for the healing of whatever needs healing.

God's very real presence acts as a kind of measuring rod or internal light for us in introspection, that enables us to interpret ourselves and our behavior when we see within. It is often, for example, a sense of God's forgiving presence *right now, at the time of looking within ourselves,* that illumines for us how far we may be from truly forgiving a person who has injured us. Or it may be during our prayer that the courage of Jesus on the cross shows us the ways in which we are bound and trapped by our own fears for our security. These are only some of the ways that prayer and Christian introspection are joined.

It would be inappropriate to give directions here on how to pray like the desert dwellers of the fourth and fifth centuries. For one thing, there is intentionally a huge variety in their prayer, for they insist at every turn that God reveals God's self to each person according to that person's needs. The monastics of the ancient world used the psalms very heavily in prayer. Past that point, some were wordy and some were silent. Some describe prayer as warfare or as very hard work. Others speak of it as a simple call for God's help and mercy in the difficulty of temptation. Still many others take the command to pray without ceasing so seriously that they devise ways of praying so that the prayer becomes integrated into the breath and the heartbeat. Others fulfill the command to pray unceasingly by giving away their meager earnings to the needy with the expectation that those who receive their charity will pray for them.

Prayer is the expression of the relationship of each one of us with God, so the structure of prayer will be different for different people. The importance of respecting that difference is what this saying is about:

> A brother questioned an old man saying, "What good work should I do so that I may live?" The old man said: "God knows what is good. I have heard it said that one of the fathers asked Abba Nis-terus the Great [this question] . . . . [Abba Nisterus] said to him, 'Are not all actions equal? Scripture says that Abraham was hospitable and God was with him. David was humble, and God was with him. [Elijah] loved interior peace and God was with him. So do whatever you see your soul desires according to God and guard your heart.'" (Apoth., Nisterus 2, p. 154)

With these cautions in mind, we will find that these Christian ancestors of ours can have something significant to teach us about prayer, and in this section I will try to draw out and interpret some of what I think they have to say for modern Christians who pray. Make use of what you can; leave for others what you cannot. Your prayer is your own, and it will be like no one else's.

To begin to pray we all need a measure of humility. We have to set aside any idea that we must be in a good or holy frame of mind in the presence of God. We must be willing to pray when we feel mean or distracted or seriously tempted and even have the intention of giving in to the temptation. We must place ourselves trustfully or even distrustfully in God's presence exactly as we are. We must relate to God in our prayer with our whole selves, and not only with our good parts. For most of us, relating to God in this way is something we have to learn over a long time. Not getting discouraged as we grow is itself an act of humility.

PRAYER, THE FUNDAMENTAL ACTIVITY

Prayer is the fundamental activity of the Christian; to be in the image of God means to communicate with God. Many people are intimidated by prayer, believing that there is a right and wrong way, and thinking that they will somehow offend God or make fools of themselves if they do it wrongly. It is helpful to know that our monastic ancestors were convinced that prayer is natural to us, like breathing, if we only discover it in ourselves. It is something we do, but even more, it is a gift of God to us. We do not even have to enter God's presence in prayer, because we are already in God's presence. It may be helpful to think not of entering God's presence, but rather of making ourselves accessible to prayer. Prayer shapes us and transforms us. It centers us in God and at the same time in ourselves. It is always changing, as we are always becoming new in God.

Nevertheless, this discussion of introspection and prayer and overcoming the passions in order to love might suggest that the primary reason we pray has to do with transformation. This is misleading, however, for while prayer makes us who we are, we do not pray in order to become new any more than we marry the person we marry primarily in order to become somebody else. We pray, first of all, to be with God. Secondarily we pray knowing that God has promised us good things which we can expect through prayer. If we let prayer be only a means to something else we want, however, it will not be for us what it can be, and we will not be who we can be.

UNDERSTANDING THE PSALMS FOR PRAYER

The starting point of prayer in the early church was the Book of Psalms. This had been true for private and public worship for a long time before monasticism developed, and the psalms continued to have a fundamental place in Christian worship throughout our period. In Egypt both the communal and private prayer of the monastics was based in the psalms. Sometimes they were recited while our desert ancestors wove mats or baskets or did other kinds of work with their hands in order to leave their minds free for prayer. Sometimes they were recited while a man or presumably a woman stood with arms outstretched to make a cross shape with the body, as was common for early prayer.

This emphasis upon the psalms can be puzzling to the modern reader who is aware of the bloodthirsty or at least vengeful nature of many of them. In the most offensive of them, the psalmist calls upon God to destroy the enemy in a particularly horrible manner; in others the psalmist gloats over the destruction of a personal enemy or an enemy of the nation. Other psalms seem to be characterized by a simple-minded conviction that the good always prosper materially while the wicked always end up paying for their wickedness. Still others seem to emphasize God's exclusive choice of Israel to be God's people, while some psalms suggest that other nations have their own very real gods who are simply not as powerful as Israel's. Little of all of this in the psalms can seem useful to the modern Christian, and a lot of it is actually embarrassing.

Modern biblical scholarship over the past hundred and fifty years or so throws helpful light on all this, however, by illuminating for us the way in which the Bible, Old Testament and New, was put together. In the picture the scholars paint, we have come to see many different parts of scripture coming from a huge span of time, for the Old Testament over more than a millennium. Some of the parts were originally passed down orally and, like the Song of Miriam in Exodus, date from the time when the people of God were wanderers in the desert. Other parts, like the central core of 2 Samuel, apparently were always in written form and date from the time when Israel was a nation. Other parts come from the time of the exile, and others take us very close to the period of the New Testament. Not surprisingly, when the parts are sorted out it becomes apparent that just as the life conditions of the people of God through the centuries were constantly changing, their understanding of God and God's ways also changed and developed, and all of this is reflected in the literature of the Bible, including the psalms. This means that most modern Christian biblical scholars hold to some kind of a notion of progressive development in which the ancient Hebrews, for example, over a period of centuries go from believing that their God was the greatest among the gods of the individual nations to believing that their God was the only God, who loved and intended the salvation of all people.

Our fourth-century Christian ancestors, however, did not believe in any kind of progressive revelation. The God Abraham and Sarah knew had the same characteristics for them as God had for the psalmist who asked God to bash the heads of the babies of the enemies on the rocks. God is God, always the same, always trustworthy and loving. Whatever contradictions or inconsistencies, whatever unworthy characteristics were ascribed to God by scripture, whatever questionable human behavior was exhibited by biblical heroes or heroines must have this logical explanation—whenever we come to an offensive or puzzling passage that contradicts what we know of God in Christ, we know that scripture is directing us to look underneath the surface to a deeper meaning. To early Christians all of scripture is true, and meant to be useful to us.

To make sense of the hard parts, they believed, we must read scripture allegorically, to use the traditional name for this understanding of scripture. God does not desire to dash the heads of any babies against the rocks; therefore, the babies and the rocks, too, must be only allegorical or metaphorical, a way of talking about how Christians are to live, or about God's promises for the future, including the promise of God's gift of Christ. Origen, the third-century Egyptian biblical scholar who developed this method of reading scripture, explains that what the psalmist must really be asking for, then, when he asks God to bash the heads of the enemies' babies, is for God to destroy the psalmist's little thoughts from which the psalmist's passions grow. When we pray this psalm, then, this is what we ask for for ourselves.

Immediately a question arises for the modern reader: is this not simply reading into scripture anything we want it to say? The answer is not as straightforward as we would like. First, those who use this method of understanding scripture really are reading into the texts what the original author never intended. Scripture *is* the accumulated and precious repository of our ancestors in the faith over a long time, and we do see that faith develop and change throughout the Bible. After all, as we are real in our prayer, so the biblical writers were also real in their time. The author of Psalm 137 really was probably asking God to kill his enemies' babies, not the roots of his passions, whether Origen thought so or not. Nevertheless, scripture is truly the book of the people of God, and there is something profoundly right about the church's insistence over the centuries that scripture is for worship and for growth in the life of God. Whatever we mean by revelation, scripture has the same ability to reveal God and ourselves to ourselves as it ever had, and often what it reveals is far more or at least far different from what its original authors intended.

As for a check on the individual Christian imagination, the ancient church insisted that allegorical reading of scripture always took place within the Christian community. While the Holy Spirit can help each one of us to ever deeper understandings of scripture, just as scripture reveals one God, that God is fundamentally the same for each of us, and intends the same fundamental life of love for each of us. In the same community one of us might experience God most nearly as judge, another as lover, and both these images belong to God as we meet God in scripture. If, however, we meet God in scripture, and God seems to be telling us that we are to execute God's righteous judgment on drunken drivers by fire-bombing their houses, it is another matter, for there is a serious discrepancy between the presumed private revelation of God and the revelation of God to God's church. The God of the Christians tells us that it is neither our place to execute God's judgment on others nor even to pass certain kinds of moral judgment on others.

This may be baffling to Protestants who have been taught that interpretation of scripture needs no more than the willing heart, the Holy Spirit, and a Bible. But scripture is the book of the church, and Christian community is the setting in which we must interpret it, for there is no Christianity that consists only of the individual believer and God. The presence of the community is a source of grace once we give up private ways of reading scripture.

In the present the psalms can have the same profound place in prayer as they had for ancient Christians when we allow them to speak for and to us, both individually and in community. Protestants especially often believe that the only real prayer is prayer that gushes from the heart in our own words at the time we pray, and because of this our prayer is many times impoverished. We may be tired or demoralized or distracted when we try to pray. At other times, we do not know how to pray or what to pray for and so we cannot pray at all. Our Christian ancestors knew, however, that no prayer is simply our own. Prayer, no matter how private, is always also the prayer of the church, and the gift of God. The psalms belong to the great prayers of the church, and when we pray them they are as truly our prayers as those we speak in our own words from our hearts. They are the prayers of the body of Christ, of which we are a very real part. We need the psalms to join us as a community, to shape us and form us, to teach us at a deep level who we are and who God is.

PSALMS IN PRIVATE PRAYER

How do we use the psalms, then, in our own private, modern prayer? Though the early monastics worked through the psalms in order, most of us find them easier to use if they are grouped according to the church's seasons and the time of day. Many modern Christian communions publish books for daily prayer in which the psalms still have their traditional importance; these prayer books can be used according to your own needs: one or more psalms a day can be used, depending on what is most helpful to you. If no prayer book is available, you might try beginning and ending your prayer with a psalm or a part of a psalm following the order they appear in the Bible.

You will be true to the intent of the ancient monastics if you read slowly, a line at a time. Let the images flow around you as your own images. Origen said that if you feel the need to stop and ponder a line or an image within a line do so. Do not hurry or strive for efficiency. Your prayer is not a chore you must complete.

Any image or combination of images may speak to you in a special way. For example, Psalm 126 goes

> When the Lord delivered Zion from bondage,
> it seemed like a dream.
> Then was our mouth filled with laughter,
> on our lips there were songs.
> The heathens themselves said: "What marvels
> the Lord worked for them!"
> What marvels the Lord worked for us!
> Indeed we were glad.
> Deliver us, O Lord, from our bondage
> as streams in dry land.
> Those who are sowing in tears
> will sing when they reap.
> They go out, they go out, full of tears,
> carrying seed for the sowing:
> they come back, they come back, full of song,
> carrying their sheaves.

Originally, this psalm was a song referring to the end of the Babylonian Captivity of the people in Israel. In the song the psalmist recalls God's deliverance from that bondage, asks for a new deliverance, and then envisions a future happiness when God's new deliverance comes into being.

There are many different ways that this psalm can become your own prayer. You may, when you say the words, remember the way you yourself have been liberated from a past terrible bondage, external or internal, and your heart may well up with a gratitude for your freedom that in the present begins to release you from a present despair or anger.

Or you may be struck, as you say the words, by a knowledge of your own present bondage to your depression or avarice or pride or anger or fear; then you are able to hear in a particular way the promise that though your struggle with it now is a kind of sowing in tears, in the end you can not only master it but benefit by it.

Or you might be reminded or even hear for the first time that the bondage from which you need to be released is a bondage created by the voices in your own head that keep you from being who you are called to be, voices which say "you always mess up everything" or "women cannot do what men do" or "shut up; you talk too much."

At many other times, that bondage you are acutely aware of may be the social forces that seem so hard to even identify, much less overcome, if we are to live in a world in which people will not die of cold or hunger or war. In these cases, as you pray "deliver us . . ." you will know that you are praying with the voice of all God's people for the world we live in.

A word of caution: at the time when a line or image in the psalm you are praying speaks to you, you may be tempted to stop there and analyze it, working out all the logical conclusions you can draw from your insight. Or you might begin to expand on the image and go off on a psychological analysis of yourself as you apply it to yourself. It is better not to give in to these urges. Do your introspective analysis outside of the reading and reflecting on the psalms, perhaps while doing chores or drinking a cup of coffee. Doing it in prayer is a kind of monopolizing of the conversation between you and God. Furthermore, you are seizing control of a process that needs you to let the images speak to your heart before they reach your head. Perhaps use a journal for working out your ideas.

When you pray the psalms, simply be there in the presence of

God and let whatever comes to you come to you. Stop if you need to, and reread the line, then sit quietly until you wish to go on. But remember, prayer is a gift, a being in the presence of God, not an exercise in analysis. In this way scripture may really be revelation for us as we become able to meet new aspects of God, ourselves, and other people we may not ever have met before.

NAMING GOD AND PUTTING ASIDE THE NAMES

Somewhere around the end of the fifth century or the beginning of the sixth there lived an anonymous theologian who influenced both the prayer and theology of the Western and the Eastern churches for centuries to come. This writer's works erroneously circulated under the name of Dionysius the Areopagite, but because we have no other name for him or her, we will use this name, too.

Dionysius was writing out of and clarifying a very old tradition that had its various roots as far back as the second and third centuries, but which really flourished in monastic theology and practice with such people as Gregory of Nyssa and Evagrius Ponticus, whom we have already met in these pages. This tradition makes a distinction between two ways of knowing and experiencing God in prayer that can be very helpful to the modern Christian: in the first way, we draw near to God as we increasingly learn more and more about who God really is for us, for God's people, and for the world. In the tradition, prayer of this sort is called *kataphatic* prayer, but Gregory speaks of it also as "calling God by name" or knowing God by means of created things. In the second way of prayer, paradoxically, we come to meet God by finding the ways in which our very real knowledge of God often actually gets in the way of our being with God and learning to set that knowledge aside. This way of prayer the tradition calls *apophatic* prayer, or "the way of unknowing."

In the ancient world, those who write about these two ways often talk as though the first kind of prayer is only a prelude to the second kind, or as though these two ways of prayer are opposites which exclude each other. This is misleading because the two kinds of prayer are not only closely related, both are essential to Christian prayer. We do not outgrow the one as we move to the other.

Calling God by Name

What does it mean to "call God by name" in this tradition of prayer? To Gregory of Nyssa it meant two things: first, to reflect upon a biblical name or image of God until we understand deeply what that name or image means about God to us, and second, to reflect upon the way in which we, as images of God and children of God, make this name or image ours by taking on the characteristics of God.

On the surface, this might appear to be a simple-minded task that we might sit down and do on a winter's evening when we have nothing else with which to occupy ourselves: we could make two lists, putting names for God in one column, and human characteristics of these names in the other. This, however, is not what Gregory and his tradition means. Learning the names for God and their consequences for us is a lifelong enterprise that may on occasion include some systematic analysis, but systematic analysis is not fundamentally at the heart of it. Learning the names for God involves the uncovering of our own passions, of our distortions of God, the world, and ourselves, and of our self-deceptions in order to discover a God, a world, and a self we have never seen more than glimpses of before. This process is sometimes painful and sometimes wonderful.

All of us who pray call God by name. In our formal prayers we address God as Father or the Almighty or Lord or Master. When we use these names or any other names, they carry images with them of who God is. At certain times some of these images seem very close to us; at other times, they do not resonate with much inside us at all, but instead we are using them only according to a convention.

Everybody would like to think that what we believe about God we believe in a fairly straightforward manner. We have been taught well in church, we take the Bible seriously, and we have carefully thought through the questions of religion. We have made our own conscious decisions about what we believe and why. Unfortunately, what we believe about God is not necessarily all that simple. We are able to make some real choices, but we may not even be aware of a lot of what we believe about God. How we understand God and orient ourselves with respect to God has come to us from many places—from things we have read or heard, experiences we have had, people we have known, including especially our parental figures.

Our relationships with these special adults were particularly influential on our deep images of God. When we were children they cared for us, loved us in their own way, seemed to know us inside and out almost magically, exercised authority over us. They lived in an adult world that operated on laws of conversation, knowledge, courtesy, and morality which often we could not understand. We learned that our parents were pleased and displeased respectively by good and bad children, and demanded obedience from us. But we also learned that God, our heavenly Father, knows everything, is pleased with good children and angry with bad children, and demands obedience. Naturally enough, God and our parent or parents ran together a bit in most of our minds, even though we never decided to make the connection. Whatever other characteristics our parents had which touched us in some formative way we probably ascribed to God, too.

Often, what we have consciously chosen to believe about God may be very unlike the images of God that formed in us as children and which are still operating in us at a deep level. For example, one person might choose to believe that God is loving. That person holds it as a real conviction, and truly believes that he knows God *is* loving. Nevertheless, he carries around in himself the feeling that he is always under judgment, that whatever he does, he never does it well enough. At a deep level he believes he has already been judged by a God who would have loved him if only he had achieved more in his life.

Another example: a woman is convinced on good biblical, theological, and personal grounds that in the sight of God men and women are equals; this woman has a good job she enjoys, a husband she loves, and a happy family. Nevertheless, she is often tortured by the feeling that perhaps she ought not have a job that she enjoys and which consumes energy she could expend on her family instead. Her feelings of self-doubt that cause her so much suffering are often baffling to the rest of her family who believe she is doing just what she ought to be doing.

In both of these cases, what they believe in their heads is battling against what is in their hearts. In the first example, the sufferer grew up with very critical parents who were hardly ever satisfied with anything their child attempted. Though he knows he is hurting himself, as an adult, he is now never satisfied with what he does. The God he believes he knows rationally accepts him as he is; the God of his heart, out of which he lives, speaks to him with a voice even more critical than his parents', and he cannot find the knob to turn it off. In the second example, as a little girl watching and listening to her parents and her grandmother, she learned that God loves good people. Without them teaching her directly, she also learned that women become good by sacrificing themselves for their families, that a good woman must not have a life apart from her husband and children, and if she does, her whole family will pay disastrously for her selfishness. Whatever she knows in her head, it is very hard to budge the deeper convictions of this woman's heart about what it means to be a good woman, acceptable to God. It does not help her resolve this internal struggle to find that the Christian tradition through the centuries has put women in a secondary position with respect to men in all sorts of ways.

This man and this woman and most of us as well are caught in some version of Saint Paul's dilemma: what I believe in my head I cannot believe in my heart, and what I do not wish to believe in my head I cannot help believing in my heart (cf. Rom. 7:9). We may pray till we drop, asking God to give us self-confidence, but if we stand before God in our hearts believing that God only accepts us when we are perfect, our prayer is likely only to lead us into the passion of depression and despair, or to encourage us to be self-deceptive and pretend to a self-confidence we do not feel. We must live out of our hearts, yet how can we exercise enough freedom to bring our hearts and heads together? How, for that matter, can we allow into our hearts what we may never have known at all?

All of us pray with something of this problem. We think that we know who God is, and yet much of what we find we believe stands in the way of our prayer and our life as well. Who wants to spend time with a God who seems to us to be only interested in us when we are successful, or who made us male or female and then seems to hold our gender against us? Learning to call God by new names in prayer is the beginning of one real way out of this trap.

When we are dealing with a specific problem, one way to go about learning the names of God in our heart is to be introspective, then do as Evagrius Ponticus suggests with what you find—"Ask Christ for an explanation." Go into your prayer time with a particular question in your mind based on what you find when you look inside, such as "why am I angry all the time?" or "why do people suffer so much if you are supposed to be so loving?" or "why am I not able to break free of my envy of others?" or even "why do I feel so rotten right now?"

If you have a lot to say to God, go ahead and say it. Tell God how angry you are and how it is hurting you, for example. But leave a lot of time just to sit quietly in the presence of God, without talking or deliberately thinking through what you have brought into your prayer. Your head will surely fill up with thoughts, of people you love and are concerned for, of chores to do, of what you will have for dinner. Do not try to push all these thoughts out of your mind. They are you, and the whole of you is coming into the presence of God, just as you are. Nevertheless, let them be there in your mind without paying much attention to them, while your original question remains in your mind as well. Do not let go of it. Evagrius says,

> Stand resolute, fully intent on your prayer. Pay no heed to the concerns and thoughts that might arise the while. They do nothing better than disturb and upset you so as to dissolve the fixity of your purpose. (E.P. Prayer 9, p. 37)

After a while during this time you will often find new images, or new ways of seeing things arising in your mind that you will be able to bring with you out of your prayer to think through at other times of the day. As you learn to practice this regularly, not only will you gain a new perspective on your questions; you will meet new facets of God as well.

We have already talked at length about praying the psalms. Praying the psalms in the way we have suggested is another one of the most helpful ways of "naming God," learning to break out of the trap to be able to call God by new names in the prayer of our hearts. Let us go back to it for a moment. We spoke of the way we sit in quiet in the presence of God and slowly go through the psalm we are praying. We are not furiously analyzing what we are reading. We try, instead, simply to be there, listening and present, knowing that we are in the presence of God whether or not we experience God's presence. After all, we know, at least with our head, that, in the words of Psalm 139, there is nowhere we could go to flee God's presence, even if we wanted to. We try to make ourselves receptive to the images of God and of God's people present in the psalm. We wait for an image to become alive for us that has never been alive before. We cannot force this to happen, but we can be actively receptive to what we read. Sometimes we can go for days without an image coming to life; we can learn not to be impatient as we remember that we are in the presence of God, and that in itself is good. Then at some point an image may come alive, and as we allow that image to unfold within us we find that we are able to begin to experience God and what God wants of us differently, that our knowledge of who God is for us grows larger and larger, that our unbudgeable hearts are changing, that we can name God with new names.

Here is one example of how this works. While she was praying Psalm 91, a friend of mine was seized by its imagery of God as a great mother eagle protecting a baby bird with her huge wings; she found herself vividly imagining herself as that scared little bird up against the eagle's feathery body, feeling well protected from her bird-hunting enemy. This entire image and the feeling that went with it was almost a completely new experience for her. My friend has always been a perfectionist, and she mostly had experienced her God in perfectionistic terms. Before this, she had known with her head that God loves all God's human children exactly as they are, but in her heart she had only rarely been able to feel that God loved her, especially when she displayed signs of weakness or fear or even minor incompetencies.

Praying this psalm did not change her image of God or of herself all at once. Prayer rarely works this way. It did, however, after her prayer for that night, start her mulling over her feelings and behavior as a child in the family in which she had grown up, and then as a mother to her own children. She thought of her childhood and her family's contemptuous pity for the weak, and she could see the way she had attributed those family attitudes to God. Later, she remembered holding her own babies, and how she had known that whatever they did as children or adults, she would love them, and love them all the more in their weakness as they needed her. As she thought of God's mothering of her she began to know in her heart that God's love of her could not be less fierce than her own for her babies. She was struck with amazement as she really knew herself to be in the presence of God's love, which was far greater than anything she had ever imagined.

As she continued her prayers over the weeks, this knowledge of God's love made her sensitive to new images and new names of God: of God the defender of widows and orphans, of God who surrounds God's people with strength as the mountains surround

Jerusalem, of God who turns our wildest and most barren places into pastureland.

Dorotheos of Gaza, when asked about the relationship between love of God and love of the neighbor, had used a diagram of a circle to explain it: if we imagine God at the center, and our lives as lines drawn from the circumference to the center, we will see that as we move closer to God, we also move closer to other human beings. Growth in the love of God brings with it growth in our love for others. What we would expect from reading Dorotheos also happened to my friend as her knowledge of God's love for her grew, and as she began to be able to love God in return. Her sensitivity to others and their needs also grew. She began to understand God, not just as her own, but as the mother, father, and lover of all human beings. She knew that God yearned with love for God's human children in the same way she had yearned over her babies. She began to be very conscious of her judgmentalism, and for the first time, she began to get free of it as she felt deeply how irrelevant any person's condition or moral state was to God's love. Some of the more painful aspects of the passions of perfectionism, pride, and envy started to fall away. In the light of this knowledge of God's love, a concern for all of God's people, but especially those who suffer from hunger or cold or loneliness or despair or the effects of war, grew within her.

Human beings are made in the image of God, and so a change in the way we are able to know and name God in our hearts will change the deep ways we understand ourselves and what we wish to be. Every new name for God carries with it a new name for us, and so we move away from our passions toward freedom and love by God's grace, and our own willingness to be receptive to it and grow in it.

The Way of Unknowing

Sitting in silence is an essential characteristic of prayer, particularly for naming God. Abba Moses tells his monks who ask him questions, "Sit in your cell and your cell will teach you everything" (Apoth., Moses 6, p. 139). Perhaps there is nothing more important that our ancient Christian ancestors have to teach us than how much we are in need of silence. In the kind of prayer we have discussed so far silence has served a purpose. It has been a silence which is a kind of waiting and listening for what God may tell us through the words of scripture, through our own hearts.

The prayer that we turn to now involves a different kind of silence, the silence we experience as we sit with a person we know very well and love. It is the silence of being in God's presence without asking for or expecting anything, but just being there. The tradition of the ancient Eastern Christian church said that we relate to God in two ways: by what we know, that is, by "naming God," and by what we cannot know. God is both knowable and unknowable. God reveals God's very self to us in the world we live in, in scripture, in Jesus Christ, in the church, through other people, through our prayer. Nevertheless, no matter how many names we are able to call God by, what we know of God can never exhaust who God is. God is beyond us, mysterious, out of our grasp, never ever in our control. We can enter into the presence of God as God is beyond us, and when we do, we know without any doubt that whatever God is, God cannot be categorized absolutely by human beings.

Mysterious as this sounds, it is not difficult to understand because all human beings, really all living things, share this double quality. Think of the way we relate to a close relative or a spouse or a long-term friend. If you are a parent of a child still at home, you probably know your child very well and love him dearly. You know how he feels about most things, and you know what he is likely to do in most situations. He may even be so predictable that you know what he will say when he is tired or in a bad mood. You know these things because you have been living in the same household for years. At some point, however, the chances are, in a conversation perhaps or when checking on him in bed, you realize that he is also a stranger to you. He is not an extension of yourself, or a composite of your spouse and yourself. Your child has an existence so different from your own that you cannot put yourself in his mind even for a minute. He is alien to you, other than you. The knowledge you have of him is real, but he lies beyond and away from that knowledge. Strangely, however, if you have had this experience, you know it is wonderful. How good it is to live in a world that is not the extension of your own mind! How good that your child has a life not in your control! How careful you know you must be to respect that distance and natural privacy of the people you love! Paradoxically, at the moment when you sensed your child's otherness, you probably also experienced a rush of love for him and he seemed then to be particularly dear to you.

Related to this is some of the good time we spend with a person dear to us without talking. Remember the common experience of being with a spouse or close friend at the end of a long day of talking or working on a project or doing chores. You know each other. You have just shared a common experience. Sometimes you want to talk about it, but sometimes what you need is not to talk at all, but rather just to be quiet together. Words seem too much. They only ride on the surface of the deep way you are together at that moment.

This is what the prayer of unknowing is about. We all need to call God by name, to learn at a deep level who God is for us, and to communicate with that God. As we spend time with God in this way, which we are at least able to talk about in terms of images and concepts, we also need to spend the other kind of time with God. We need to be with God without thinking about anything, imagining anything, or asking for anything. We want to be in the presence of God as comfortably as we are with a person we love with whom silence itself is a kind of communication, as delightfully as we are with the person with whom we are in love.

The Christian mystics through the ages have tended to speak of this prayer in terms that turn away ordinary Christians like ourselves. Evagrius called it pure prayer, because it was free of words and concepts, and he said that it only followed a long apprenticeship in the other kinds of prayer. Gregory of Nyssa speaks metaphorically of it as knowing God in the darkness, where the first kind is knowing God in the light, and he, too, suggests it is experienced only by the heroes of prayer.

I believe that the tradition has been misleading, however. God is so close to us that God is never such a total stranger with whom we must become acquainted that silent time together is without meaning. All who pray are able to spend time with God in this way each day. Each of us can take time during prayer, whether only a few moments or much longer, just to sit and be there quietly in the presence of God, asking for nothing, saying nothing, thinking about nothing in particular, but just aware of God's presence.

Chapter 6

God

A knowledge of God cannot be taught or learned apart from living out a life that is a reflection of who God is. This is the first principle of the early Christians we have been considering. Knowledge of God does not consist of a set of answers to a list of questions. It is more like the way a wife knows her husband, or a husband knows his wife. The knowledge husband and wife have of each other includes a profound respect for the otherness of the other; based in love, each seeks to preserve the integrity of the other, allowing the other *to be* without simply becoming an extension of the spouse. It is a knowledge that comes out of living together, responding to each other's daily interests and needs, being shaped by deep caring for the other. It is a transforming knowledge.

We have pondered our ancient sources as they have instructed us about love itself, and about humility, the passions, introspection, and prayer. We saw that prayer puts us in the presence of God. But if we try to look directly now at God, what are we able to see?

GOD IS LOVE

First, God is love. God loves beyond our dreams, extravagantly, without limit. Whatever we might imagine God's love for us to be, it is far deeper, steadier, gentler. It cannot be manipulated or bargained with. It cannot be earned or lost. In the words of Psalm 125, it surrounds us as the mountains surround Jerusalem. It fills the whole creation with light. It shines with a kind of joy in the heavens, and it illuminates each blade of grass, each tiny bug, opening our eyes to see them. It is the air we breathe, the ground we walk on, the food we eat.

This love draws us to God in ways we know and in ways we do not know, for God made our universe in such a way that everything created is attracted to God its creator and lover. Nothing exists whose deepest being is not turned toward God. Everything that exists only becomes what it is meant to be as it moves toward God. The movement toward God is the movement of the planets and the tides, the sun and the moon, the birth, growth, and decay of animals and plants, the loving movement of human beings toward other human beings. "Our hearts are restless till they find their rest in you, [our God]," says the fifth-century writer, Augustine of Hippo (*Confessions*, Book 1, Chap. 1). Only in this movement toward God is there rest.

Each of us moves with that attraction in a different way according to the variety of God's universe, and God is first known to each of us according to our own history and our own needs. We may begin with an unspecified longing, a curiosity, or fear, or a sense of God's goodness in creation, perhaps even a dread of judgment. If we do not choose to turn aside from this movement, and if we choose this rest, we find that we all are moving together into an ever-increasing love not only of God, but of all that is.

Choosing to move toward love may not seem possible or realistic to you. Many people, perhaps even most people, have been so wounded by their experiences of life that love itself seems to be an illusion. The idea of such love of God is baffling to the person who has never experienced love. To the person who has only experienced love mixed with pain, coercion, and humiliation, love may not even seem desirable. For many people who grew up in a tradition in which we were told that God loves us in spite of our being nothing better than worms, God's love has in the past seemed to demand that we give up any shred of self-esteem or claim we might have for our own needs. An image of God's love as healing may look at best like wishful thinking or sentimental nonsense.

Part of the power of the early monastic image of this love lies in the understanding of the way we become aware of this love. A few of us can never remember being without a consciousness of it. Others of us met it in our childhood in crippled form—we were loved perhaps by people who loved only out of feelings, not by disposition. So very many of us began to learn about love slowly and painfully. It might have begun at the moment we received an unexpected gift of kindness or courtesy. Something we read may have given us a glimpse of what love might be like. We might have been struck by a view of love we did not know existed in a stranger we accidentally encountered. Everyone who knows love can tell stories of this kind. Everyone who learns to love as a disposition learns it over a very long time, a whole lifetime. The love with which we begin to love may very well be as crippled as that which we receive. It is nevertheless a start, and it is real. Nurture it, think about it, desire it. If you can, pray for it. Sudden conversions to love can take place, but only very rarely. That is not the way our God usually works.

This is meant only to give you encouragement to trust the glimmers of love you have almost certainly had and which you will still receive. God's love already surrounds you, even if you cannot feel it. Trust just a little; listen attentively. Try to call for help to the God you may not know, and be quiet for a moment. If you are able to extend one small act of kindness to another human being or an animal, you have already begun to live out of that love. If you feel you cannot yet pray, try anyway. Speak your anger or despair to God and begin to think about where love is to be found. Love will not come to you without in the end your own choosing. Love must be sought out and cultivated in yourself. Remember Anthony's answer to the brother who asked Anthony to pray for him:

> I will have no mercy on you and neither will God have any, if you yourself do not make an effort and if you do not pray to God. (Apoth., Anthony 16, p. 4)

God loves us too much to wish us passively to receive whatever life sends. God will not cram even love down our throats unless we choose it, seek it, learn it.

The movement toward God is the movement from the circumference of Dorotheos's circle to God who is the center, and it is God who defines the circumference. It is the character of God that defines what it means for us to be human, but what this character is we can know truly only as we dimly see it, recklessly try to make it our own, and boldly ask God for the transformation of our hearts. This character is love.

The love of God is particular. It is like the sun which shines on everyone, the good and bad alike, but it also comes to us, if we are willing to receive it, in a way exactly suited to each of us, as we are able to thrive on it. It is the love of the God of Psalm 139, who knows all our bones and sinews, who knit them up together, who knew us in the womb, and who knows that part of ourselves hidden even from us. In the present, it has the power to raise our own particular dry bones and clothe them with flesh (Ezekiel 37). It pours out on us like rain on dry ground, and makes even the pastures of our wilderness fertile (Psalm 65).

In a particular way this love appeared among us in Jesus Christ, from whom the love of each Christian who belongs to the body of Christ flows. It has been passed on in the beginning from Christian to Christian, and from Christian to God's world. This same love is God's for us, us for each other, and us for the world, just as we are and just as the world is, in all its beauty and its imperfection.

THE HUMILITY OF GOD

Humility is a primary virtue for the monastic. It is a state of mind, an attitude of heart that allows a Christian to love. It undergirds and makes possible all the other characteristics of Christian love. We have called it a relational virtue, because it always positively shapes our feelings, thoughts, and behavior toward other people and God. Like everything else which is good, it springs from God.

The first ingredient of God's love is God's humility. All of God's dealings with us are marked by the humility of God we see so amazingly in the incarnation itself. The depth of this humility is simply beyond our imagining.

> . . . Just as neither the ages above nor the ages below can grasp the greatness of God and [God's] incomprehensibility, so also neither the worlds above or the worlds on earth can understand the humility of God and how [God] renders [God's] self little to the humble and small. Just as [God's] greatness is incomprehensible, so also is [God's] humility. (Mac., Homily 32, p. 180)

Humility was an offensive characteristic for a God, in the eyes of early non-Christians. How could Christians worship a God who deliberately chose to share in human birth with all its mess and vulnerability and limitation, as well as a shameful death? How can we now worship a God to whom all the unimportant little details of our lives actually matter? How can we respect a God who takes us more seriously than we take ourselves, and yet is not impressed with all our accomplishments? Who loves us equally well, whether we succeed or fail? How could it really be that God simply dis-regards not only our education, our tastes, our industry, our nice-ness, our worthiness in order to love us? God's greatness we can begin to approach. The sheer humility of God's love is incompre-hensible. Some of us turn away from such a God in disgust; others overlay such divine humility with the arbitrary power and despotic might they find more appropriate to their God.

God's humility overturns every pattern of human relating that would allow us to cut ourselves off from others, even in the most subtle ways. All of us stand in the same position relative to that divine humility. We cannot love and learn of God even in our prayer unless we learn to approach others without pride. We must learn this obvious truth over and over again.

> They said of an old man that he went on fasting for seventy weeks, eating a meal only once a week. He asked of God the meaning of a text of the holy Scriptures and God did not reveal it to him. So he said to himself: "Here I am: I have worked so hard and profited nothing. I will go to my brother and ask him." Just as he had shut his door on the way out, an angel of the Lord was sent to him; and the angel said: "The seventy weeks of your fast have not brought you near to God: but now you are humbled and going to your brother, I have been sent to show you the meaning of the text." And he explained to him what he had asked, and went away. (Say. 72, p. 171)

God's humility is incomprehensible, but it draws us in an un-derstandable way with love. We feel its gentleness and its refusal to bully us or violate the integrity of our choices. It does not need to threaten us with God's power. Indeed, it is seeing the humility of God that makes us recognize that that sense of coercion we often feel, to be or do something we cannot do, is not God's power at all, but something destructive in ourselves or around us that we have taken on ourselves in spite of God.

God's humility says "be humble as I am humble." As we see it we imitate it, and as we imitate it, we learn something deeper of it that draws us all the more. Humility is not a heaviness, but a lightness. "My yoke is easy, and my burden is light" (Matt. 11:30). It is a gift. It is a delight. We bathe in it, and we extend it to others. We learn through it to give up our pretensions with others, and so we enjoy the best of all God's good gifts: the gift of knowing people, not as we need them to be, but as they really are.

GOD WITHOUT PASSIONS

A passion is a strong emotion or state of mind that blinds the one whom it possesses, making it impossible to see anything or anyone, even God, as it really is. A passion is destructive by definition. It takes away choice; it makes the unwholesome look wholesome, and the good, insipid. Ancient Christians insisted that our God is and must be in this sense without passions.

Being without passions, God sees us exactly as we are, that is, with the clarity of love. Only God can see us so well and so deeply, so "reasonably," for to see reasonably is to love. Because God is without passions, we need not stand in God's presence in fear. The passions of pride and anger, fear of the future, even the passion of vainglory have no place in God. God is not enslaved by avarice, lust, depression, or pride. Because God is without passions, God does not see us through a haze of uncontrollable longing that warps even eternal vision. God sees us, and God loves us utterly, as we are loved by no one else.

Because God is without passions, God loves us steadfastly. God is faithful, and we can count on this faithfulness because God is not at one time angry with us, at another time in a good mood. God is never arbitrary, never acts on a whim. This does not mean that God is, therefore, predictable to us in the way a predictable human being might seem to be, because we never know in what form we will meet God's steadfast love. God cannot be manipulated. What we can know of God, however, says Gregory of Nyssa, while we question everything else is this: God comes to the help of those in need.

This passionlessness is not just one quality of God among many that are equal to it. It burned in the heart of God in the crucifixion. As Jesus suffered blinding pain, God was not blinded. God saw the cruelty, carelessness, and misunderstanding that led to the crucifixion, and God knew exactly what God saw. Only God could see the human hearts of the crucifiers, and so the words Jesus spoke, "Father, forgive them; for they know not what they do" (Luke 23:34), are the words of Jesus the human being who was the very image of the God who loves, humbly and without passion.

The ancient monastics also wished to be without the passions that blinded them to the wounds and vulnerabilities of other people. They wanted to love, too, to heal the hurts that keep us from God and each other.

Three old men, of whom one had a bad reputation, came one day to Abba Achilles. The first asked him, "Father, make me a fishing-net." "I will not make you one," he replied. Then the second said, "Of your charity make one, so that we may have a souvenir of you in the monastery." But he said, "I do not have time." Then the third one, who had a bad reputation, said, "Make me a fishing-net, so that I may have something from your hands, Father." Abba Achilles answered him at once, "For you, I will make one." Then the other two old men asked him privately, "Why did you not want to do what we asked you, but you promised to do what he asked?" The old man gave them this answer, "I told you I would not make one, and you were not disappointed, since you thought that I had no time. But if I had not made one for him, he would have said, 'The old man has heard about my sin, and that is why he does not want to make me anything,' and so our relationship would have broken down. But now I have cheered his soul, so that he will not be overcome with grief." (Apoth., Achilles 1, pp. 28–29)

As Achilles was concerned not to wound or discourage the brother at the very time he was most unworthy, so God is concerned for our own healing when we hurt ourselves and others out of our passions.

TO LOVE AS GOD LOVES

Early Christian monastics desired with their whole hearts to imitate this love which drew them toward God and toward others so that others would also be able to know this love and live out of it. For them, God's love, their love of God, the love of God extended to them through their communities, and their love with which they desired to love others, all these were the same love. God's love was primary; out of God's love for them flowed all other love. In God's communities they were the body of Christ.

We also truly are the body of Christ. The line that separates God's love for creation and for other human beings from our own love is hard to find because our love *is* a part of God's love. This does not mean that the love of God is "simply" human love given some mystical meaning. It does mean that we want to love well. We want to be living embodiments of God's love, as Jesus was, and as our monastic forebears wanted to be. This is what it means to be the body of Christ.

This is what all that we have talked about up until this point has been about. Being a Christian means learning to love with God's love. But God's love is not a warm feeling in the pit of the stomach.

It has definite characteristics we learn in the course of our life, in the behavior and teaching of the early monastics, as we ponder over what we can say about God as God deals with us, and finally, as we model our own lives on what we have learned.

The love of the monastics was also extravagantly patient and extravagantly hopeful, based as it was on the patience and hope of God. Repeatedly, the younger ones are told by the older to be patient with themselves, to know that they would not finally have to live in the grip of their passions, but also not to expect that their passions would be rooted out overnight.

Many of their stories illustrate the realistic nature of this patient love when it is extended to others:

> One of the old men said that he had heard holy men say that there are young men who show old men how to live: and they told this story.
>
> There was a drunken old man, who wove a mat a day, sold it in the next village, and drank as much as he could with the money. Then a monk came to live with him, and also wove a mat a day. The old man took this mat as well, sold it, bought wine with the price of both, and brought back to the monk only a little bread for the evening meal. Though this went on for three years, the brother said nothing.
>
> At the end of three years the monk said to himself: "Here am I, with little enough bread and nothing else, I will go away." But then he had second thoughts, and said to himself: "Where can I go? I will stay here, and for God's sake continue this common life." And immediately an angel of the Lord appeared to him, and said: "Don't go away, we shall come for you tomorrow." That day the monk begged the old man: "Don't go anywhere: today [the angels] will come to take me away." At the time the old man usually went out to the village, he said to the monk: "They will not come today my son: it is already late." The monk used every argument to show that they would come: and even while he was talking, he slept in peace. The old man wept, and said: "I am sorrowful, my son, that I have lived in neglect for so many years, and you through patience have saved your soul in so short a time." And thenceforward the old man became sober and serious. (Say., p. 179)

This is not a story about the necessity of allowing yourself to be destroyed in an abusive relationship. It is not a story to use to tell an abused wife to stay in a marriage that is killing her. Instead, it is a powerful story about the way in which the Christian sticks to the task undertaken, believing in the power of love to transform the human heart. The important detail in the story is that the monk died without knowing the outcome of his work. Even at the very end, the dying monk asked the old drunk to stay with him while he died, and the old man did not intend to stay. The man died, never knowing what would finally happen, but also not grieving over the old man. The monk might not have seen a transformation in him, but he knew that if one was to come, he had lived the best way he knew how to allow for it. Whatever happened, he knew that he, and all people, live out of and in the love of God. He had lived and died like Jesus, who also did not know the outcome of his own death.

This exercise of patience and hope rises from the deep springs of the knowledge of God's love for all that God has created. It is letting go, knowing that in God's universe, finally, God will be all in all.

> As near as the body is to the soul . . . so much nearer is God present, to come and open the locked doors of our heart and to fill us with heavenly riches. . . . [God's] promises cannot deceive, provided we only persevere to the end. . . . Glory be to the compassionate mercies of [God] forever! Amen. (Mac., Homily 11, p. 82)

Select Bibliography

The following English translations are all available to the modern interested reader. The letters in parentheses are the abbreviations used in the text.

(Ant.) *The Letters of Saint Anthony the Great.* Translated by Derwas Chitty. Fairacres, Oxford: Sisters of the Love of God Press, 1975.

(V.A.) Athanasius: *The Life of Anthony and the Letter to Marcellinus.* Edited by Robert Gregg, Classics of Western Spirituality. New York: Paulist Press, 1980.

(Dor.) *Dorotheos of Gaza: Discourses and Sayings.* Translation and introduction by Eric P. Wheeler. Kalamazoo, Mich.: Cistercian Publications, 1977.

(E.P. Prak.; E.P. Prayer) Evagrius Ponticus, *The Praktikos: Chapters on Prayer.* Edited by M. Basil Pennington. Translation and introduction by John Bamberger, O.C.S.O. Spencer, Mass.: Cistercian Publications, 1970.

(Gr.Life) Gregory of Nyssa: *The Life of Moses.* Translation, introduction, and notes by Abraham Malherbe and Everett Ferguson. Classics of Western Spirituality. New York: Paulist Press, 1978.

(Gr.OP) "On Perfection" in *Gregory of Nyssa: Ascetical Works.* Translated by V. W. Callahan. Fathers of the Church 58. Washington, D.C.: Catholic University of America Press, 1967.

(Mac.) *Intoxicated with God: The Fifty Spiritual Homilies of Macarius.* Translation and introduction by George Maloney, S.J. Denville, N.J.: Dimension Books, 1978.

(V.P.) *Pachomian Koinonia. Vol. One: The Life of Saint Pachomius and His Disciples.* Translation and introduction by Armand Veilleux. Kalamazoo, Mich.: Cistercian Publications, 1980.

(Pal.) *Palladius: The Lausiac History.* Translation by Robert T. Meyer. Ancient Christian Writers 34. Westminster, Md.: Newman Press, 1964.

There are many collections of the Sayings of the Fathers which have survived from the early church, in Greek, Latin, and Syriac. Of the two collections I have used here, the Ward translation is from a Greek text in which the sayings are grouped together under the names of the mothers or fathers to whom they are attributed. The other text, translated by Chadwick, is in Latin, and the sayings are grouped according to topic.

(Apoth.) *The Sayings of the Desert Fathers: The Alphabetical Collection.* Translated by Benedicta Ward, S.L.G. Oxford: A. R. Mowbray, 1981.

(Say.) ''The Sayings of the Fathers,'' in *Western Asceticism.* Selected translations and introductions by Owen Chadwick. Library of Christian Classics. Philadelphia: Westminster Press, 1958.

on "love"
& "God"